All the Rage

All the Rage

A Quest

Martin Moran

Beacon Press,
Boston

Beacon Press
Boston, Massachusetts
www.beacon.org

Beacon Press books
are published under the auspices of
the Unitarian Universalist Association of Congregations.

19 18 17 16   8 7 6 5 4 3 2 1

This book is printed on acid-free paper that meets the uncoated paper
ANSI/NISO specifications for permanence as revised in 1992.

Excerpts of this book, in slightly different form, originally appeared in
Ploughshares and in *Pushcart Prize XXXV: Best of the Small Presses.*

Text design and composition by Kim Arney

This is a work of nonfiction. It is also the work of dreams and memory.
Some names and identifying details have been altered to honor the
privacy of individuals.

Library of Congress Cataloging-in-Publication Data
Moran, Martin
All the rage : a quest / Martin Moran.
pages cm
ISBN 978-0-8070-8657-5 (hardback)
ISBN 978-0-8070-8677-3 (ebook)
1. Moran, Martin—Childhood and youth. 2. Actors—United
States—Biography. 3. Sexually abused teenagers—United States—Biography.
4. Child sexual abuse by clergy—United States. 5. Forgiveness. I. Title.
PN2287.M6993A3 2016
792.02'8092—dc23
[B]
2015034264

For David Francis Moran
Beloved Brother, Teacher, and Poet
1965–2009

Dear Reader,
I'm longing to tell you about a dream I had.
But first,
Let me tell you what happened,
while apparently awake.

ON A FINE SPRING DAY, WANDERING through a New Orleans bookshop, I came upon a sentence, part of an interview with the writer Richard Ford. It was framed upon the wall like a prayer, a diploma.

"Life can be seen to be about almost nothing else sometimes than our wish for redress."

A short time later, wandering the World Wide Web, I stumbled upon a phrase printed in florid cursive, like a wedding invitation or a message of condolence. It was a quote by the late peace activist and journalist Norman Cousins.

"Life is an adventure in forgiveness."

In Ford's words I heard the voice of hardboiled truth—the human plight of eye for an eye. In Cousins's, the lilting cadence of the grade-school nuns who conveyed the creed of being a good soul.

Both phrases struck me as accurate, as linked. Seemingly different quests—redress, forgiveness—aren't they born of the same urge, to mend what we think broken, to put to rest the reverberations of having been wronged? To land us, at long last, back home?

THE DOCTOR IS AN OLDER MAN, soft-spoken. He moves with an unhurried gentleness as he takes Siba's hand and welcomes him.

He turns and asks if I've done this before. I tell him it's my first time.

"Well, we'll go easy," he says. "If we have to pause or you don't understand something, just say so. We'll stop if need be. Please tell Siba we're in no rush here."

He smiles and gestures for us to sit.

I arrange the folding chairs as taught in my recently completed course, Introduction to Interpreting. The teacher at the International Institute, a Russian émigré, had explained how it's best to organize the space so that the client and doctor face each other and you, the interpreter, are off to the side. "It's best when you disappear," she'd counseled. "And keep your boundaries. Remember, you are a shared tongue, nothing more."

In English the doctor asks Siba,

How are you feeling today?

And I translate.

Comment allez-vous aujourd'hui, Siba?

Ça va, merci. Mais, j'ai mal à la tête.

OK, thank you. But, I have a headache.

Just today or often?

Juste aujourd'hui ou souvent?

Souvent.

Often.

One small window allows a bit of sun into the cramped room: a steel desk, a counter with jars (Q-tips, tongue depressors), an exam table, the chairs in which we sit, a trashcan marked

"Biohazard." My heart bangs against my ribs and I smile at Siba, who seems perfectly calm. The doctor looks up from his clipboard and says,

"Tell me what happened."

Siba explains quietly, his wrists in constant motion, how he'd left his wife and child in the city to go to the countryside in order to visit the town of his birth. How his boyhood friend invited him to a village meeting where they discussed the need for clean water and schools. The situation had become unbearable. There were many sick children, and men were being arbitrarily arrested, accused of being antigovernment rebels, disappearing. They talked of making contact with a human rights organization. Suddenly, in the midst of their discussion, soldiers rushed into the courtyard of the meetinghouse. They began shooting. Some were killed; others escaped. Siba was thrown against a wall, handcuffed, and blindfolded, stuffed in the back of a truck. Two days' dark journey, no food or water. Then, a prison. There he was questioned and tortured until, one lucky morning, he escaped.

After all the telling, the doctor asks Siba to please move to the exam table and take off his shirt and pants. He asks Siba if he is comfortable with the interpreter remaining in the room. Siba glances at me, nods, and removes his clothes and sits, slump-shouldered, his legs stretched out before him. Sunlight falls across his face.

The doctor holds a yellow measuring tape across Siba's back, between his shoulder blades, as if fitting him for a new suit. He is documenting the length and breadth of each scar. The doctor measures, then pauses to make notes. This is the evidence the judge will need, the reasons and the proof written on the body. These notes will be attached to Siba's I-589, a Department of

Homeland Security Application for Asylum and for Withholding of Removal.

Sometimes the doctor touches a particular mark and asks,

"Now, is this from the wooden club, or was this from the broken glass?"

I translate and glance out the window toward the Metropolitan Opera House, toward the clear sky of a February morning in New York City in the year 2008.

"They put the glass in the crooks of your arms, your knees?" the doctor asks as he points to the back of his own knees, trying to get a handle on this method of extracting information. Siba nods and describes how the glass was shaped, how they bent and bound his limbs around the glass. He says,

"They tightened the ropes; they kept yelling questions, beating me about the head and back until I passed out."

"This happened how many times?"

"Four."

"Did you always lose consciousness?"

"Yes. Each time, I woke up back in my cell."

I WAS STANDING IN THE LIVING ROOM of my Manhattan apartment holding a receiver attached to a phone wired to the wall. I was glad for the grounded line, the grip of the thing, as I heard myself say,

"Could you please connect me to the police, the police station for Goleta, California?"

It was early in the year 2006. Drifts of muddied snow were dwindling in the warmth beyond the window. I was unaware of having crossed from my desk through our living room to pick up the telephone. It happened as if in a dream, yet now the real voice, the flat vowels, the well-mannered melody of a middle-American operator:

"Please hold, sir, for the Goleta Sheriff's Department."

"Thank you, ma'am."

The public school kids were out in the sun across the street. Jackets tied at the waist, tossed to the foot of the fence. My eyes stayed out the window toward the sky-blue day, the swirl of little bodies on the playground, as I waited for the cross-continent connection. Waited through a distant crackle, then a long stretch of silence linking itself to the law of the land in California. I'd been at the desk paying bills? Composing sentences? Now, suddenly, pressing the receiver to my head to keep from hanging up, a thumping heart betraying an old fear, an old ache to make right what went wrong.

It was ringing.

I pictured a small town. Rural. Never been there. I knew it only as the return address scribbled on a long-ago letter sent to me by Bob. I had no idea if he still lived there, if he still lived.

It was ringing and a tantrum rose up in my chest: *Hang up!* Questions hammered: *What are you afraid of? The derision of a sheriff? That you're betraying your old buddy Bob? That he might hurt or threaten you? For Christ's sake, you're nearly fifty, kid. Talk about Stockholm syndrome.*

"Hello. Sheriff's office."

It was a woman on the line and I was instantly relieved. What I wished to say I thought would be easier to reveal to a her. She repeated,

"Sheriff's office."

"Hello. My name is Martin Moran and . . ." My voice quavered from whiskerless boy to man of fifty. "I am calling because I think someone may reside there who molested me when I was a kid."

I was conscious in that instant how news of my friend Ben's death, some months before, was part of the impetus for this call, this reaching back. What happened to Ben was more brutal, I figured, than what happened to me. At least Bob hadn't plied me with liquor and fucked me in the ass. Nonetheless . . .

"Yes. How can I help you?" the sheriff asked.

"I just wanted to be sure that you were aware of his . . . him."

How matter-of-fact I suddenly sounded.

"Was he ever convicted?" she asked.

"Yes, ma'am. In Colorado. In the seventies," I said, thinking (again) how someone *else* did that brave work. "Not by me, though, ma'am."

I heard my voice lilting upward against the weight of an adage (the heft of Edmund Burke) lodged in my brain somewhere along the way:

The only thing necessary for evil to triumph is for good men to do nothing.

Nothing is what I had done.

Easy now. You were a kid, kid. You were a kid.

"His name?" she asked.

"Robert Kosanke."

I said it aloud to her and I type it now for you (for me) in black letters on a white page. Tabloid style.

Robert Kosanke.

The name. The real, the actual, the seven-letter nonfiction name.

In my memoir released in 2005, I recounted the story of my sexual entanglement with Kosanke. "Bob." The guy who pulled me into his sleeping bag at a boys' summer camp a few months after my twelfth birthday, the illicit sex ending when I was a freshman in high school. I also created a stage version of my story, a dramatic monologue rendering the essentials: Catholic upbringing, the molestation at twelve, finding and confronting Bob thirty years later. In the book I called him Robert C__. I didn't want to ruffle any feathers, to sully my poetry with his sullied name. I didn't want a harangue but an inquiry. And I liked (still do) the space, the invitation for readers to fill in the blank with their very own ghost, their private nemesis. And the little dash of emptiness—of mystery—reminds me of the stories of an earlier time ("Josef K__. was dreaming. It was a beautiful day and K__. felt like going for a walk."), by an old-world author like, for instance, Kafka. The tiny void that hums of a dark tale, a fable that reminds you how you'll never quite know, never totally understand, the whole story. Even if you're the one who lived it, the one who's attempting to remember, to tell it. I believed that without the weight of his factual name, without the business of blame, the

narrative could rise toward the grace and forgiveness it was seeking. That's what I wished (then) and that's what I set out to com-
pose: a kid's hymn to freedom, a man's ode to compassion.

And besides, the publisher's legal counsel felt it prudent to
alter identifying names and details. Ah, a comfort to have my
Catholic school courtesy, my aesthetic choice, seconded by
literary-legal opinion.

OK.

So.

Here I am now, spelling out *Kosanke*. And I confess that doing so rings a bit of belated redress. Is this the bitter thrill of
vengeance, I wonder? An admission of my abiding desire for payback? Do I like the idea that somewhere, someone who knows
him (he himself?) will feel the sting of seeing the true name in
print? Even as I worry the sting will hurt others, him, or even as
I wonder if stinging him is part of freeing me and fuck it. Is that
what I'm after at this late date? A step, a stab, a slap that I missed,
a jot of justice that will help to put the whole mess to rest?

If so, so be it.

Or, is this ink you now see (this phone call I recount) simply
a long-deferred civic duty? A small but important effort to protect others?

"Still checking," the lady said. I heard the clicking sound of what
must be her fingernails on a keyboard. I imagined a small street,
a ramshackle house; a truck in the drive up on a jack, missing a
wheel, tools scattered in a driveway, weeds creeping through
cracked cement. I pictured him gray and slow and bent, as he was
when I finally found and faced him one afternoon in 2002 at a
VA hospital in California. He told me then how he fixed up old

cars for a meager living and I imagined him now asking a neighbor boy to help change a tire on the old Chevy, to step inside for a spot of lemonade.

"Yes . . . yes he does live here," she finally said.

"So he's alive?" I asked, amazed that a phone call was all it took to confirm this fact and disappointed, I realized, that he wasn't dead. Always guessing that death (his or mine) would be the certain period on this story. This story that apparently (for here I am *again* at the keyboard typing "Bob") refuses to end.

"Yes, we know where he is," she continued, with a kind of Perry Mason delivery. "He is a *registrant.*"

"What's that?"

"He's required by law to register with us periodically. It's part of his agreement. He is current, I see."

"So you're aware, I mean, able to—"

"Yes, sir. We keep an eye."

The relief! Someone was doing the job of stopping him. The job I never did. How many slim, blond boys came after me? How many like Ben?

"Anything else I can help you with?"

"Ah, no. No. Thank you so much. Thank you."

"Well, thanks for your call, Martin." Her voice was kindness. "Take good care, now."

My throat tightened, my eyes welled up.

She understands, I thought. *She understands everything.*

It took me thirty years to call the cops.

SIBA KEEPS SHAKING HIS HEAD as if pushing away an unwanted vision. His chest is heaving, tears spilling down his cheeks, but he is silent, choking back any sound.

"*Respire*," I whisper. "Breathe." I don't know what else to say.

We've just stepped out of a psychologist's office, his second required medical interview. He told his story, yet again, laid it all out for another affidavit to be filed in support of his case. He spoke of his dream to see his family again; then, abruptly, the session ended. The doctor's time was up. Now we're out on the street, and as we walk I'm thinking of what an asylum officer once said about deciding cases such as Siba's:

"I have to feel pity for them. That's all. They need to make me cry or I'm likely to deny their claim."

We are heading west on East Eighty-Sixth Street, the leafless trees of Central Park a few blocks ahead. It's February and frigid. We move through the midday glare, the crowd weaving around us, all suits and purpose. We pass under a green awning; a doorman in a long coat studded with golden buttons. For the briefest moment I raise my right hand and place it against Siba's back, between his shoulder blades. I dig into my jacket pocket, come up with a crumpled napkin. He takes it, presses it to his nose, and wipes his eyes. Then he stops suddenly, near the corner of Park Avenue, and looks down at the gleaming sidewalk.

"What? What is it?" I ask.

A woman clad in fur, her poodle on a leash, steps around us.

"*Si je n'arrête pas...*" he pauses, chokes the tears. "*Si je n'arrête pas de pleurer, je deviens aveugle.*" "If I don't stop crying, I will go blind."

"Oh, *ce n'est pas vrai*," I tell him. "It's not true. Crying won't make you blind. Tears are OK, helpful. Tears are . . ."

But what do I know? I hear my awkward French drift off into the cold. I wonder who might have told him such a thing, if he means it as literally as it seems he does. I wonder what it might feel like to know that how well, how convincingly, you tell your story could be the difference between sanctuary and deportation, between liberty and a forced return to peril.

Siba lifts his head and we continue on, crossing Park Avenue.

THE PLACE I CALL HOME sits on the high ground of northern Manhattan on a narrow stretch of street dubbed Cabrini Boulevard. It is named for Saint Frances Xavier Cabrini, patron of immigrants. Better known as Mother Cabrini. The first American citizen to be canonized. That was in 1946.

My husband, Henry, and I moved into this apartment in the spring of 2000. We're both actors who work primarily in the theater, so it felt (still feels) rather miraculous that we managed to purchase a little slice of New York real estate. We'd had a three-year stretch of well-paid jobs and so our tax returns gave the necessary impression that we're solid enough citizens to be allowed a mortgage. So far, so good.

Our place is a cozy one-bedroom, a "junior four" they call it, perched on the second floor just across the skinny boulevard from an elementary school. PS 187. The sweet and anxious parade of parents dropping their kids at the school door—quick kisses, final waves, epic backpacks strapped to tiny bodies—accompanies our morning coffee. The sights and high-pitched shouts of recess punctuate the weekday hours at my desk.

Yesterday, for example, I looked up upon hearing a rumpus and caught sight of two boys, sixth graders, I'd guess, midconflict. A tall and tough-seeming skinny kid, chest thrust forward like a cocky cock, was yelling. Indistinct, but full-throated, yells. I watched as he yanked a sweatshirt from the grasp of a squat, fat kid. He taunted the chunky boy who, nervous and red-faced, held perfectly still. Their schoolmates turned from their games and began to encircle the conflict. Their voices, the taunting and the tension, rising. And then, in one sudden blast of rage, the heavy boy's arm flew out and across the cheek of the tall, cocky kid, who went straight to his knees, covering his face. I was astonished at the force. The suddenness. Within seconds, a teacher was on them. She whisked the two students inside.

Why aren't you more angry about what happened to you?

I was asked this question (in several ways by several souls) after I told my story of reconciliation in the form of a book and a play. It's a simple enough question that has, beyond all reason, grown into an obsession, a quest, a riddle demanding an answer. A circling maze of circling queries craving, it seems, to pinpoint a certain . . . knowing? A truth?

It's vexing though not uninteresting to discover that, like a mathematician, you're living inside a problem that offers clues but does not necessarily wish to yield up an answer.

Does every convex polyhedron have a net?

Go figure.

IN 1975 I HAD A TEACHER named Brother Tom. My freshman year of high school. He was one of the youngest among our Jesuit instructors.

We were far enough into the year to have already plodded through the Old and so were making our way through the New Testament, which thrilled him, apparently, because after months of being slumped at his desk while we slogged through all those begets and all that wrath, the Gospel stories had him up and circling us fifteen-year-olds, bouncing on the balls of his feet imploring:

"You see how gorgeous this idea? This *turn the other cheek?*"

Sometimes he'd pick up a large crucifix and kiss the feet of the Corpus.

"You see how radical this *do unto others* is? What vision, what strength this took? Who was this Jesus come into the world to alter our consciousness?"

He'd look at us with his rheumy eyes, rub his little mustache, cuddle the crucifix, the good book.

Brother Tom loved what he called "healthy debate."

"Was it proper for a Catholic leader, a priest like Father Berrigan, for example, to march in the streets against the Vietnam War?"

"Should our school go co-ed?"

Mostly, ever fearful of ruffling feathers, I kept quiet during these heated discussions. One morning it was something simple.

"Which of the four Gospels strikes you as most effective, Mr. Moran?"

"Oh, um . . ."

Not wanting to offend, least of all a dead apostle, I said something like,

"Gee, they're all pretty good."

And the usually mild-mannered Jesuit snapped.

"Enough with all the *nice*, Mr. Moran. Speak up, for Christ's sake! Get some spine."

His face was suddenly red, his body tense, his voice a slap. His eyes were locked on mine. He was angry. I stared down into the sacred text, the ink swimming. And when finally I looked up to meet his eyes again, the frightening flash of them had softened to concern and he said, very quietly,

"Show me someone *always nice*, Marty, and I will show you someone sitting on a mountain of anger."

SHORTLY AFTER MY MEMOIR WAS LAUNCHED, in June 2005, an article appeared in my hometown newspaper, the *Denver Post*. A reaction to the book.

I offer a few lines:

> . . . when a story hits that close to home, you mumble something about the grace of God and then you get angry. Even though Moran does not. I still cannot understand how strangely protective Moran remains toward Bob. Moran refuses to print his real name, he said, because he does not want to cause him pain. But because the man is a convicted sex offender I told Moran I would—Robert C. Kosanke. . . . Most troubling is Moran's continued reluctance to despise or even blame his molester. . . . Makes one wonder if he will ever truly move on. . . .

When I opened the newspaper to a little photo of me at twelve and read the ensuing review, I am embarrassed to report that it knocked the wind out of me. I felt unhinged, *unmanned*. Though I found the writer's comments presumptuous, though I knew somehow they had much to do with him and less to do with my work, his words pained me in ways I barely understood. It was as though from amid the black ink had come the howl of a village elder:

"Grow a couple, Moran!"

I walked around for several hours (I *hate* to admit, weeks, months, still?) feeling humiliated.

I knew the man who wrote the article. We had attended, though at different times, the same Denver Jesuit high school.

He'd interviewed me extensively in 2004 when the one-man-play version of my story was opening in New York. And now, I sensed that he in some way wanted, *needed* the book version to render some form of justice in response to the foul crimes committed in our Catholic boyhood community—the unforgivable offense of messing with a kid.

What I felt (rightly or wrongly I will never know) was the reviewer's outrage that I dared not cry out in full-throated condemnation in the course of the book. And even though I knew that censure and finger-pointing was not what I was interested in, not what I wrote, his reaction left me with the feeling that I had failed in some profound way. As man, as writer, as artist? Perhaps worst of all, that I had left an important component of the human story unexamined. My human story.

I should have been able to cast this aside, surely—one man's rather self-righteous point of view. I am a grown-up. A performer used to being critiqued. The fellow at the *Post* was a good man and was doing his job; I was doing mine. And, as my father, a newspaperman, used to say, the article would soon be at the bottom of a birdcage. Let it go.

But it niggled. No, it stabbed. Did I skip, am I frightened of, an essential step on the road to wholeness? Did I leap too swiftly to forgiveness? Am I avoiding, *not even aware of,* my own buried rage?

And I must admit that he was not the first to question a lack of fury in my tale as told. At discussions after I read from the book or perform the dramatic rendering of my story, often enough an audience member will raise a hand:

"But . . . Mr. Moran, where is your anger?"

It could (and still can) bring blood to my face, a puzzling wash of anxiety that must stem, I am figuring, from the fact that they've hit a tender mark. That I've failed to dig deeply enough, that this very human emotion has been left unexplored in my work. Nay, my soul!

That I am, dear God, not *finished* with this fucking story.

You'd think that an award-winning three-hundred-page book and (he says modestly) the award-winning run of an Off-Broadway solo show would do the trick.

Closure.

Liberation.

Peace.

"Mr. Moran, where is your anger?"

The question pisses me off.

NEARLY EVERY DAY ON MY WAY TO CATCH the subway I pass Cabrini High School, and the steeple of Mother Cabrini Church. She's up there, cast in bronze, overlooking the parking lot and in a dark drawing nailed to the front gate.

Her official title is Virgin Foundress of the Institute of the Missionary Sisters of the Sacred Heart. Her corpse (minus her head, which is somewhere in Italy) is encased in glass beneath the church altar right across the street from where you catch the A train. There's a gift shop there where a soft-spoken saleslady will describe in detail how Mother founded sixty-seven schools, hospitals, and orphanages all across the United States and beyond. Mostly, mind you, by horse and buggy.

Holy mackerel.

I often find myself dashing across the street to avoid Cabrini's dark eyes. Her fierce face has become a dare. If I pass too closely, I hear a little Italian lilt; I glimpse a bony finger rising up.

You.

Who me?

Yes, YOU. What are you doing in the world? What impact before you die?

Jesus, lady, lay off.

The year was 2007. I was nearing fifty, and Cabrini's query had managed to finger a growing turbulence within. A fear that I'd mislaid what I once thought was ambition. Purpose. That I'd lost my way.

For over three decades I'd been making my living as an actor. (I *know*; I'm lucky.) I'd spent most of the past two years banging two halves of a coconut together to create the clomping sound of a horse as I pretend-galloped around the stage at the Shubert Theater. I was playing Sir Robin, one of Monty Python's knights on a quest to find the Holy Grail, in the Broadway musical *Spamalot*. Sir Robin, the knight who poops his pants at the least sign of danger.

Perfect casting.

It was a dream job, donning a wig, prancing and singing on Broadway, eight shows a week.

"How are you tonight?" colleagues will often ask as you step into a theater to sign in for the evening show.

"I'm living the dream!" is an oft-heard stage-door reply.

I *was* living the dream. This is what I thought I always wanted. Yet a deep and troubling restlessness had been rising. A sharp sense that I was wrong, somehow, that I lacked something essential. That there was a bigger, deeper endeavor I was meant to be . . . endeavoring. Out there in the worldly world. If only I could figure it out, harness the full extent of my power. If only I could be stronger, more effective.

WHEN I WAS SIXTEEN, ALMOST SEVENTEEN, I encountered, for the first time in my life, what I feared was hatred for another. The force of it terrified me.

I'd just fled the all-boys Denver Catholic high school where I'd spent freshman year and switched to the local public school, George Washington High. It was a way to distance myself, I think, from the culture that brought me a Bob and that reminded me daily I was damned

After some months of adjusting, of quietly negotiating the mammoth halls teeming with girls and boys of every size and color, I found some footing and went into overdrive to take on the role of a straight-A, club-joining, All-American Public School Boy.

By the end of junior year, not only was I elected "Head Boy," class president, but I also found myself playing Jesus in the spring musical, *Godspell.*

One afternoon, my recently divorced father called to tell me he was bringing his new friend to see me play Jesus. He wanted me to meet her. So that night, right after curtain call, as soon as I could get out of my Christ costume, I headed for the school lobby. Who, I wondered, was this gal going to be?

They were standing near the large portrait of our first president. Her hands were folded, a large handbag dangling from her wrist. She had, I noticed, the exact same hairdo as George Washington. Though hers was dyed red. The second I laid eyes on her it was immediate: a terrifying antipathy. My God, I thought, she's so loud, so large, so alien, with so much makeup and so many cigarettes.

Her name was Barbara and it turned out that she lived in Dad's condo complex across Leetsdale Drive not far from school and it was there, in the community room, over vodka tonics, that she'd met her new neighbor, my dad. Some months and several cocktails later, they announced their plans to wed.

I knew this was my dear father's bid for happiness. A happiness he certainly deserved. He'd been crushed by my mother's insistence on a divorce, the dissolution of his dream: to keep his family and his suburban lawn well groomed and in one piece. I understood that he wanted this new relationship but I just could not reconcile his being with this person who, between puffs, bad-mouthed my mom or barked at us for not eating our green beans.

I knew she had been through some kind of hell. She'd lost her father when she was very young, had grown up with a demanding and difficult mother, had gone through her own tough divorce. I *felt* for her even as I abhorred her. Being in her presence was like entering a storm where waves of disgust met with flashes of pity. The power of my feelings around her frightened and shamed me.

Not long after finishing up my stint as Jesus, I was over at Dad's, and on an impulse I took the elevator three floors up from his studio apartment to hers and knocked. Surprise. She looked rather shaken at the sight of me and I understood—President Jesus calling.

She gestured for me to sit, lit up a Virginia Slim, and said, "What do you want?"

"Barbara, it looks like we're going to be . . . family. Maybe we should try to . . ."

She pointed two pink nails, the two featuring a fuming tip, right toward my face, fixed me with a stare, and said,

"You know something? I've got your number."

I felt a sudden panic; my face froze into a silent grimace. She continued,

"Yeah. You're a big, fat phony."

My throat clamped shut. Her eye, her keen eye, conveyed that she saw right through Head Boy, straight to the tainted secrets: my disgust for her, my already checkered past, my paralyzing crush on each and every member of the boys' basketball team. She blew her smoke and I muttered something like,

"*Jesus* Christ."

"What did you say?"

"Oh . . . I . . . nothing. Take care."

I left and, not quite intending to, slammed the door.

And so it began: the Thirty Years' War. Or, the Cold War. A lifelong string of tangled disputes. For example, one night after she and my dad had retired to Las Vegas (after I'd already pissed her off by flipping over the George W. Bush photo stuck to their fridge), I made the mistake of bringing up the gambling issue. She stood suddenly and glared at me.

"Please calm down, Barbara," I said as I raised my hands and fought to quiet my voice. "All I'm saying is that the gambling could bankrupt you and Dad and. . . ."

Her face went white and she stormed from the room. I was banished: two years in Siberia. She wouldn't speak to me.

Another evening—this was during my college years—we were having Chinese at an all-you-can-eat buffet in San Francisco. When Dad went off to the loo, she leaned forward, cigarette in hand, and whispered,

"You have something to tell your father, don't you? You want me to just say it? You're a homosexual. And how, I wonder, could you do that to your family?"

I ran and found a pay phone, got ahold of my shrink.

"The thing is . . . OK, look, I mean I think this is like . . . *hatred*. I think I actually *hate* her. It's so huge, this loathing. It's not like she's a Hitler, but I'm imagining a hatchet to her head. Or, machine-gunning her. It's totally frightening! What is this?"

She-shrink said,

"Perhaps this fury is an invitation."

"An invitation to what? To kill her?"

"No, to awake. To grow."

IT WAS LIKE A WILDFIRE raging. It ignited deep within a thicket of secrets and was now leaping forth, gobbling up venerable rectories and churches and cities and the many lives in its path. The revelations of abuse by clergy exploded in New England in early 2002 and spilled out in blazing ink and news reports all across the country. Across the globe. The skeletons and injured souls tumbled out of closets. In Boston they were screaming for Cardinal Law's head. Before the year was out, he would sink in the muck, in the vast evidence of crime and cover-up. When I opened the newspaper and read of the brave speaking up after years of silence, I stood in awe, adrenaline thumping.

I cannot say if it was due to the cascading scandal, to the visceral repulsion I felt upon glimpsing a news clip of pale-faced, backpedaling bishops, but one morning late in the winter of 2002, I jotted a note and sent it to an address I had tucked away. A return address scribbled on a very old letter from Bob, sent from a town somewhere in Southern California.

I'd had no contact with him for years, had heard rumors once back in the late seventies that he'd been sent to jail. I thought he was probably dead now. In my mind, in any event, I had buried him a thousand times in a thousand different ways but . . . but . . .

The notion, it seems, had been swimming all along in the crevices of my unconscious, formulating in the frontal cortex—

Find him.

Face it.

Man up.

I jotted the note, dropped it in the mail on my way to catch the A train, and, basically, forgot about it.

I CAUGHT SITE OF A SKULL ON A SHELF the other day. One of those phrenology noggins—a blank-faced model of a human head upon which our beloved *sapiens* brain is colorfully mapped out. As if to suggest our mind is a continent full of little kingdoms, identifiable fiefdoms of behavior. That certain bumps and regions along the human pate pinpoint sovereign states of our emotional and cognitive proclivities. "Benevolence," "Animal," "Firmness," "Reflective," "Moral," "Acquisitiveness," "Wonder," "Sublimity," "Aggression."

Seeing the funny little head at the store was a reminder of a naïve but noble science that was all the rage in the nineteenth century. A reminder of how our thinking about our thinking has continued to evolve into ever more sophisticated forms of neuroscience and anthropology.

I realized how much this simple model appealed to me. The possibility of figuring us out with a color-coded map. Left hemisphere mathematician, right hemisphere artist-author. Over here above the ear, this is the country of memory. And next to the temple, that's where human compassion resides. You see, my savage and saintly self can be reduced to a simple fraction: I may still be three parts ape but look, I'm at least five parts angel. I'm evolving. Aren't we all?

This meditation over a colored cranium put me in mind of my quest to understand anger. So, modern genus *Homo* that I am, I Googled and came upon "Physiology of Anger," Harry Mills, PhD, and found a description of a region called the amygdala. Here's some of what the doctor offers.

Emotions more or less begin inside two almond-shaped structures in our brains which are called the amygdala. The amygdala is the part of the brain responsible for identifying threats to our well-being, and for sending out an alarm . . . that results in us taking steps to protect ourselves.

The amygdala is so efficient at warning us about threats, that it gets us reacting before the cortex (the part of the brain responsible for thought and judgment) is able to check on the reasonableness of our reaction. . . .

As you become angry your body's muscles tense up. Inside your brain, neurotransmitter chemicals known as catecholamines are released causing you to experience a burst of energy . . . [the] desire to take immediate protective action . . . Your heart rate accelerates, your blood pressure rises, and your rate of breathing increases. . . . Increased blood flow enters your limbs and extremities in preparation for physical action. Your attention narrows and becomes locked onto the target of your anger. . . . Additional brain neurotransmitters and hormones (among them adrenaline and noradrenaline) are released which trigger a lasting state of arousal.

You're now ready to fight. . . .

Our brains are wired in such a way as to influence us to act before we can . . . consider the consequences of our actions. . . . It means that learning to manage anger properly is a skill that has to be learned.

In other words, it takes practice.

THE I-589 IS TWELVE PAGES LONG. You can download it at the US government site online.

Department of Homeland Security: Application for Asylum and for Withholding of Removal. *

(Formerly, Withholding of Deportation.)

The first question on the application is,

"What is your alien number?"

The second asks if you have a Social Security number and, if so, to please write it down. It is on the third line that you are finally asked your name. Your full "last" and complete "first" name.

I leaf through the twelve pages trying to imagine a situation in which I was compelled to fill out such a form. To have to flee my own home, a land where my life was in grave danger. To have reason to be given an Alien Registration Number. To be called an "alien" in the first place. Perhaps I'd have memorized this number, like a tattoo etched on my mind.

What if I needed to ask to be Withheld from Removal, if I had to figure out what that Orwellian phrase, that limbo, actually meant in relation to my living on Earth?

I try to imagine Siba filling in the following spaces left blank for his pen.

Provide a detailed and specific account of the basis of your claim for asylum or other protection.

1. *What happened;*
2. *When the harm or mistreatment or threats occurred;*
3. *Who caused the harm or mistreatment or threats; and*
4. *Why you believe the harm or mistreatment or threats occurred.*

Then there are boxes asking for check marks.

Is it because of?

- ❏ *Race*
- ❏ *Religion*
- ❏ *Nationality*
- ❏ *Political opinion*
- ❏ *Membership in a particular social group*
- ❏ *Torture Convention?*

A FEW MONTHS AFTER I SENT THE LETTER to Bob, a letter upon which I had scribbled "Please Forward," I was in Los Angeles to visit my goddaughter, poking around for acting work.

It was a late afternoon in early April 2002. I remember this moment, this sequence of events, vividly. Or I believe I do. They are embedded in my psyche and I have written about it all before and am doing so now, again. As if rehearsing the memory, or a memory of the memory, attempting to get to the bottom of the scene from yet another angle, another point in time. Memory alters over the years, they say, with forgetting and reimagining, and that seems right but I'm telling you here I am, trying to pin the damn thing down—the *truth* of it—and, OK, I was driving down the Hollywood Freeway that April day when my cellphone beeped. A message. I pressed the button and listened. It's him. My God, that's *him*, my brain blared. Bob. And it all came rushing back—a wave through the body from groin to gullet—the fact of his existence, the fact that I'd actually sent the man a note, given him my cell number. The fact that he lives in me still as some sort of growl in the gut and now there's a message in a timeworn voice telling me that my letter was forwarded to the hospital in Los Angeles where he's recuperating from surgery.

I pulled off the freeway into a 7-Eleven parking lot. I collected myself, deep, deep breaths and, after several minutes, dialed his number.

IN 1976 AS MY PARENTS GEARED FOR DIVORCE, I was lurching toward seventeen, my chin on fire with acne, my heart with secrets.

I came home from school one afternoon, dropped my bike in the garage as usual, and looked up to see a stuffed duffle bag (Dad's, army-issue, the one I packed for summer camp) hanging from the rafters. He'd just moved out of the house. Seeing his bag dangling there was an odd reminder of his absence.

I stuck my head into the kitchen. Mom was at the sink and I asked,

"Hey, Ma? What is this?"

She came to where I stood in the door, yanking a yellow earring from her lobe.

"Oh *that*. That's my punching bag, honey. I can come out here and scream it all out as loud as I damn well please."

I stared at the green blob, strung up like a corpse.

"Ma, who is it that you want to hit?"

"Oh, it's not like that, honey," she said. "It's not some*one*. It's . . . *everything*."

Then she said—and I took this to be a major life clue— she said,

"To be truly *free*, honey, you've got to get in touch with your anger."

Sometime later I went out to the garage alone. The bag hung there like a sleeping dragon over my little brother David's paper route bike. I was sure Dave had smacked the thing. He slept in the bunk above me. I loved his little snore. It was sweet, like him. But his daytime moods were alarming. I'd once seen him punch a hole through our closet door. *He* was tough. I faced the blob, raised a fist but . . . I froze.

I couldn't exactly say why, but it had to do with terror. A fear that if I started to punch, I wouldn't be able to stop. That, like nuclear fission, the force unleashed would feed on itself, that one blow would turn into a thousand; ignite a hidden monster, an inferno that would consume the garage, our house, our church on the hill, all the known world. Me.

ON THE FEBRUARY DAY WE meet for the first time and step into the doctor's office, Siba looks so calm. I hold a blank pad, a pencil, and a small Larousse French-English dictionary in my lap, terrified that my French isn't up to snuff, that my faulty translation could somehow undermine his case. After a long silence, the doctor looks up from his clipboard and says,

"Please, tell me what happened."

Siba speaks quietly at first, his wrists in constant motion as he recounts his visit to his native village, the gathering he attended.

"*Alors, j'étais dans mon village natal, un rendezvous chez un ami. Nous avons besoin d'eau fraiche, une école pour les enfants. Plusiers enfants malades, et les hommes ont disparus, les arrestations arbitraire et violent, nous étions désespoir parce-que . . .*"

Trying to scribble down words I've missed or don't understand, I raise a hand and say,

"*Plus lentement s'il vous plait . . .* Please, slow down. OK?"

He nods.

"*Oui, oui, nous étions désespoir parce-qu'il y avait . . .*"

They were desperate: scores of children dying, no fresh water, no schools. Men were disappearing, arbitrarily arrested. Siba explains how his tribe is viewed as a threat by the ruling clan.

"*Tout à coup, les soldats sont arrivés, les explosions et chaos . . .*"

Suddenly, soldiers arrived, shooting. Everyone scattered, some escaped.

"*Les explosions et mon ami . . .*"

Siba's best friend . . .

"*Mon ami . . .*"

Shot dead, next to him.

He's incredibly still as he speaks, as tears just leak, his breathing shallow. I watch his face. He becomes most anguished, it seems, not when describing the physical abuse or the realization of his friend's death, but when he recounts the *not being believed.*

"They are so *angry.* I tell them I am not a rebel soldier. I'm your brother—not your enemy. But they do not *believe* me. They won't look at me. They won't listen."

His eyes blaze as he says the words: *they do not believe me,* as if shocked all over again in the telling. The hurt writ on his face is palpable, seems to shake the room. I can't know this, but it strikes me that for him this is the instance of betrayal, the loss of innocence. The fracture that splinters a life, sends it into exile. They do not *see*; they are not conscious of him as human. He is an object, the enemy. And this, it seems, is what scars him most of all.

Or am I projecting this, I wonder. Simplifying? I am so aware of wanting to draw lines, find connections between his life and mine. I, too, experienced betrayal, Siba. You see? Different, of course, but a rupture, a banishment. It was the moment, I think, the demarcation of life before and life after. Or am I making this up? This idea of a preexisting condition? Is there ever really a pure *prior,* a true innocence before we are marked by life?

And what is this need, I'm wondering, this desire to compare our narratives, to discern our common plight? Am I simply a voyeur? What can I truly know of Siba's experience? This man from the other side of the world, a distant culture, a different skin? He's been tortured, for God's sake. He's recounting his story so that he might find a place where he can exist in peace. He is seeking asylum.

What am I seeking? Is it a wish to witness the resiliency in him that might shed light on my own resilience? Am I trying to be of service, to do something good? Or to improve my French? Am I just busy here trying to save myself?

"GO AHEAD. GO AHEAD! HIT ME. Fucking hit me like you want to!" My little brother David's face was scarlet, his words a roar. He was backed up against the kitchen wall, my fist inches from his beardless, seventeen-year-old face. "Beat the shit out of me! Go ahead, Marty! Go fucking ahead and hit me! You know you want to!"

I was housesitting for my friend Sani in a beautiful coastal town in Maine. It was the summer of 1984. Dave flew out to visit. I made my life in the East and David lived out west, but we always managed through the years to find each other across the continent. We'd come together to hike, to visit a gallery, or ski, or discover a new hot spring where we could smoke a joint, float in our brotherly nakedness under the stars. This was our two-man fraternity, a lifelong exchange of flannel shirts, of scattered thoughts, our bodies recalling fledgling years sharing a bunk.

We were still young that summer, I twenty-four, he nearing eighteen. He needed to get away from Denver, from Mother. He hadn't yet gone off to his mountain college. He wanted to see Maine, talked of climbing Mount Katahdin.

I was using Sani's Subaru and one afternoon a few days into Dave's visit (enough days for us to be igniting each other's nerves), I was about to drive into town when I suddenly saw that the car was not in the driveway. I panicked. I discovered the keys were gone from their usual spot on the table and David was nowhere in sight. He'd taken the car without asking. He'd never driven it before, never said a word to me about it. I couldn't believe his hubris, his rudeness. I stomped around the house fuming until I saw him pull up in the Subaru station wagon a half hour later. The second he walked in the door I lashed out.

"What the fuck?"

"I went to get ice cream, dude. No big deal."

"No big deal? That is *not our* car. You did not check with me!"

"What's the problem? Calm down."

"*I'm* responsible if anything happens."

"Nothing happened. You're so uptight. Chill for once."

His obliviousness infuriated me and, apparently, my existence enraged him. Like some chemical collision we erupted and the next thing I knew I had him pinned against the wall, my fist raised, and there was his full-throated howl—

"Hit me. That's what you *want*. Do it! Come on."

"Stop it," I screamed.

"Everyone *knows* you're not a saint!"

"What the . . . ?"

We were nose to nose, my wrath naked, Dave's eyes brimming with tears. Where was this coming from, this crazy blaze?

"Hit me!" he screamed again. "*I deserve it.*" His breathing was sharp and quick. My fist shook just above his face as a fear, a force, held it back. Dave's tears began to spill. "Go ahead," he said again, his voice gone quiet. "I know you *hate* me."

It was a slam to the chest—his words, the look of pain in his eyes. There was no air in the scorched place we'd arrived. I dropped my arm and turned away. Walked outside and up the street.

We never spoke of it again. But I remember how, for the remainder of that visit, we circled each other, like bruised lovers, careful and quiet and gentle. I remember how much I wondered then, and I still wonder, at the suddenness of the inferno. My brother, whose sullen anger often frightened me, had witnessed a rage in me more violent than I had ever seen from him. I think of it now, this battle of ours, with an ache of guilt. And with gratitude for the intimacy.

A FUNNY THING HAPPENED early in my junior year of high school. I tripped upon the drama room and became a Hero. It seemed a quirk of fate, quite inadvertent, that my feet carried me to the door, that my hand took the pen and added Moran to the list of students wishing to audition for the school musical. I had some inkling, I guess, that this might be a way to shine, and so to save myself. I got the part. Suddenly, I was to play the role of Hero in *A Funny Thing Happened on the Way to the Forum.*

I remember my mother asking,

"What time will you get home from play practice?"

What did she think? That I'd suddenly joined the basketball team?

With the air of a newly minted and slightly haughty thespian I cried out,

"Ma, it's not *practice*. It's rehearsal!"

In one way or another, I've been rehearsing for Hero ever since.

"ANGER GIVES CLARITY," I heard a teacher say one day.

Such a positive thought! And, again, I was assailed by a sense that I could never get to the bottom of it. Never fully understand anger's workings, its appropriate function in human life. I dug for definition.

According to my Webster's, the first known use of the word is from around the fourteenth century.

Old Norse: *angr* (grief)

Old English: *enge* (narrow)

Latin: *angere* (to strangle)

Greek: *anchien* (to choke)

This root made sense to me. I thought of how the throat clamps shut, the face goes red when you scream bloody murder.

The word has both transitive and intransitive forms.

To make angry. To *become* angry.

Yes, to become anger itself.

If I unleashed the fury, it's me who'd get strangled? No?

I thought of the well-meaning doctor who spoke to me in gentle tones years ago about my suicide attempts. The taking of the pills, the aiming of the rifle at my head. About how these acts were "anger turned inward." His words rang hollow back then. Had no meaning whatsoever. But as the years have unfolded, so has the truth of his diagnosis.

It wasn't that long ago on a terrifyingly anxious day that I unearthed from the depths of my belly an utterly panicked and pissed off kid trying like hell to punch his way out into the light. There he was, so shockingly present in my consciousness, in the fabric of my gut. A slim boy with a mop of brown hair craving life and love and all twisted up in the sad grasp of predation. I greeted him with as much tenderness as I could muster. He made it crystal clear that until he was honored for all he'd endured, he'd keep aiming his rage right at his own black heart.

We finally shook hands. There was a good deal of sobbing and even a chuckle, followed by a restful if fleeting embrace.

I believe we're on our way to working it out. I mean . . . here we are.

It would appear that this business of forgiveness, for self and others is, indeed, an ongoing adventure.

ONE WINTER NIGHT IN LATE 2007 after a performance of *Spamalot*, I ducked past the autograph-seeking crowd at the stage door—easy to do when you're not famous from TV and when you wear a crazy wig on stage—and headed for the subway. If you dash you can catch the last uptown A express, which is usually packed with cello cases and chatty show folk who've run from their dressing rooms, faces still painted, wig caps tucked beneath baseball caps.

Amid the crush of my subway car that night, I happened to spy an old friend, Erika, a spotlight operator at one of the Broadway theaters. I called out,

"*Bon soir*, Erika."

She waved me over and I managed to squeeze in next to her.

"I haven't seen you in *très longtemps*," I said. "Ça va?" On the occasions we happened upon each other we tended to practice our Français as we tunneled uptown. She replied,

"*Oui, ça va. Merci. Et toi, Martin?* You look . . . you look terrible, Marty. Are you OK?"

"Oh, had a rough show tonight. At curtain call, when I took my bow, I saw a lady sitting all alone in the front row and she was sobbing. Just sobbing as the whole place was belting out, you know, "Always Look on the Bright Side of Life." I took one look at her and burst into tears. Frankly, Erika, I don't know what's going on. Do you ever feel that existence is passing and you're failing to understand the meaning of . . . locate the essential . . ." A torrent of words poured forth and finally I put my head in my hands and said, "I just feel lost. Crazy. Maybe the way you do when you're fifty and find yourself riding a pretend horse every night."

Erika laughed. I looked up at her. She was nodding, her eyes bright as if to say she totally understood and, again, my words tumbled.

"Maybe it's working in fantasyland eight shows a week, you know? While the actual world, the news unfolds. My God, twenty minutes with the *New York Times* can just undo you. Guantanamo, waterboarding, the Congo, the melting caps, the rising seas, the soldiers twenty-two years old, twenty-three, thirty-three . . . gone! And there I sit in a comfortable chair sipping a coffee feeling utterly disconnected and complicit, somehow, wanting to *act* but . . . you know? What are we doing? *What is going on here?*"

My tears were coming. Erika looked freaked. So I changed the subject.

"And *you*, Erika, how are *you?* I haven't seen you in *so* long. Where've you been?"

"I just got back from the Ivory Coast," she said. "Been working with refugees there. An incredible experience!" She was beaming. "I worked as a logistician for Doctors Without Borders."

"A what?"

"A logistician. Someone, not a doctor, obviously, who helps with all the practical aspects of running a Doctor's Without Borders refugee camp."

And I blurted, because it was true,

"My God, Erika! I have, seriously, always thought of doing *something*, just like . . . where is that again?"

"West Africa."

"Yes, something like that! Something *real*, and helpful to people who've *really* been through . . . you know . . . ?"

"Well," she said. "Marty, what's to stop you?"

When I got home that night, I went straight to the Internet and, forgoing the usual trance-inducing sights, I looked it up. It was there, just as Erika had said: a beautifully designed website for Medecins Sans Frontieres. And in one box, with red lettering, there was a message:

Urgent Call for French Speaking Support Staff

They were in need of volunteers, it explained, to work for six to nine months at refugee camps in far-flung places like Cameroon, Congo, Ivory Coast.

This is it! I thought. This is the *answer*. I can put all these years of studying French to good use. I can be saved by doing good works.

I filled out the application.

A few weeks later on a sunny afternoon between a matinee and an evening performance, I was summoned to the Doctors Without Borders Chelsea headquarters for my interview. I wore a button-down shirt and a great-big smile. I found myself sitting at a large conference table across from a serious woman with shortly cropped and graying hair. She was, I felt sure, an ex-nun. She tested my French. That went OK. Then she asked,

"Do you have any experience with pumps or plumbing?"

I shook my head.

"Electricity?"

"Umm, no."

"Do you have experience managing groups of people?"

Oh dear, I thought, this must be like a *job-job* interview.

"Well, I was president of the Catholic Youth Organization. I directed *The Sound of Music* in Raleigh."

Stone-faced, she nodded and then switched on a video about the latrines, the malaria, the joys of life in a refugee camp. I watched feeling sure of how rich and positive my contribution would be. The moment she turned off the video I blurted out,

"Ma'am, I'm certain I can handle this."

She put a multipage, multiple-choice test on the table along with a number two pencil, pointed to it, and left the room. I stared at it for a long time. It contained questions along the lines of:

—When filling out a purchase order the correct designee for the . . . ?

—If the shelf life of canned peaches is x months and you have twelve cans for y . . . ?

—The equivalent measurement of meters to feet when calculating the . . . ?

—When installing software on the hard drive of . . .

I could not deduce a single answer. My head throbbed. I squirmed like a fifth grader. Finally, I just colored in all the little dots at random. When she returned and looked over my work she asked,

"Mr. Moran, have you ever labored in close quarters with others over a long period of time with the real threat of death all around you?"

"Well," I responded, "have you ever worked out of town in a troubled new musical headed for Broadway?"

I laughed. She didn't. She squinted at me and then at her Birkenstocks. A letter of rejection arrived shortly thereafter, thanking me and politely expressing concern that, possibly, I lacked third-world experience.

AS I SAT THERE IN THE GLARE of the 7-Eleven parking lot, just off the Hollywood Freeway, I kept dialing part of Bob's phone number and hanging up. Finally, I managed to punch all seven digits and let it ring through. He picked up. It was astonishing how much the sound of his "hello," the melody of it, was *exactly* as I remembered. It tripped a land mine, a blast in my chest. I began imagining some version of his bespectacled face with three decades added. We carried on a very brief, businesslike conversation during which he gave me instructions on how to find him amid the sprawling hospital complex off Sepulveda Boulevard. I hung up. I sat for a moment, then got back on the highway.

The meeting was set for the following Thursday, April 4, 2002. The thirtieth anniversary of our first sexual encounter, I realized, would be that very week, April 7. How very odd, how fucking poetic. I was forty-two now and he sixty-something. Here it was, then, my grown-up chance to . . . to what? To get even? To let him have it?

My therapist, more than once, had asked,

"What would you *want* from such a meeting? I think it's important to know."

And here it is, it's going to happen, and I thought: I still don't know how to answer that. I don't know what I want beyond a face-to-face reply to one simple, nagging question—

What were you thinking, man? I was twelve.

Don't know beyond one simple desire. I want to lay eyes on the evidence. I want to look it in the eye and say,

This happened. Right? It happened.

And see the evidence nod.

Would this "set things right?" That's the meaning of *redress*, they say. "To set right, to make up for, to remedy. To heal." I see that redress can also mean *avenge*. How intriguing.

Avenge and *heal* share billing under one English term.

Maybe that's all I'm doing here. Coming to terms.

NOT LONG AFTER I HAD RECEIVED THE REJECTION letter from Doctors Without Borders, I met my friend Sara Kahn for lunch. Sara, a writer, a therapist, a terrific soprano, had pursued an acting career in her twenties and early thirties and done well. But she felt a lack, a void. She felt there was something other, something more that she was meant to be doing in the world. She left the theater, went back to school in social work, and was now employed, among other assignments, as a consultant for Doctors Without Borders. By now she'd already traveled to many turbulent regions of the world. Her life was full. She planned eventually to earn her doctorate.

We met at a small café on the Upper West Side of Manhattan. It was a rainy afternoon. I shared with her my disappointment about the rejection letter, my sense of purpose-lost midlife meltdown.

"Hey!" she said. "You don't need to go to the Ivory Coast to be of help. Have you looked out the window, at our city? Schools? Shelters? One of the places I work is the International Institute of New Jersey. We always need volunteers. Especially interpreters who can work with refugees, survivors of torture who are seeking asylum."

Our lunch, her words, made a distinct impression.

Nine months later, on a February morning in 2008, I find myself leaving the apartment at 8 a.m., exotically early for a stage actor, with a file in my hand. It contains an I-589. It is stamped with an Alien Registration Number and a young man's full legal name: Mahamat Siba Moustala. I've been instructed to get downtown to Saint Luke's-Roosevelt Hospital to meet Siba and the doctor who will conduct his first required medical interview. The day is clear and cold. I walk briskly up Cabrini Boulevard and round the corner to head to the subway. When I pass Mother Cabrini, I flash the file.

Down the steps and onto the A train. My God, it's packed at this hour. Who knew? Commuters are huddled over headlines printed in Polish, English, Spanish, Chinese. Faces from Ecuador, Moscow, Haiti, Honolulu, all swaying beneath Harlem. I find a seat between a young man in beige corduroys who wears a yarmulke and a brown-skinned schoolgirl in a plaid skirt, studying her geometry. As we jostle down the track, my leg continually bumps the knee of the Jewish scholar beside me. He is deep, I see, into Pinter's *The Birthday Party*. I observe our knocking knees, our identical joints. A million years of design, perfectly hinged bones, passed down to us. A thousand knees knocking, rocking, right on down the A line.

I notice an ad across from me. It features a chubby-faced, balding man with a tight-lipped grin, the knot of his striped tie snug against his Adam's apple. These words are pasted next to his pasty face:

Deportation? Green Card? Immigration Questions?
1–800–Immigration or 1–800–Innocence.

I study the file in my lap, turning to the section that contains Siba's declaration, his reasons for fleeing Africa. This is the story he will repeat to countless officials. And his case has to be strong. Since the passing of the Patriot Act, Sara told me, gaining asylum has become far more difficult. I study the text and flip through my French-English dictionary, looking up words I don't recognize.

Where exactly *is* Sudan, I wonder. Chad? There are, I recall, miniature maps of the world in the back of my daily calendar. I dig it out from my bag and turn to the great continent. Chad is orange, just below a purple Libya, next to huge Sudan, touching green-colored Cameroon. Africa looks like a Milton Bradley board game, a children's jigsaw. And, oh my, look how tiny Togo is. And Zimbabwe is all the way down near South Africa! Who knew?

I feel like Sarah Palin cramming for an interview.

At 125th Street a woman bursts on to the train. She wears a wool skirt, sensible shoes; her hair is knotted into a fierce bun. "Cruelty free planet!" she cries. "Cruelty free!" She makes her way through the crush handing out colorful fliers urging us at the top of her lungs to "Stop the slaughter! Stop eating meat!"

"Stop the yelling," says a woman opposite me who is reading *Eat, Pray, Love.* I take a flier from the screaming lady, who won't meet my eye, and study the glossy pages.

Printed across the top of the pamphlet is a row of little, though famous, disembodied heads. Grinning celebrities with quote bubbles floating up from their lips.

"*They feel pain, just as we do.*" Joaquin Phoenix.

"*It is up to us to stop the massacre.*" Carrie Underwood.

"*If you could feel or see the suffering, you wouldn't think twice. Give back life. Don't eat meat!*" Kim Basinger.

I tuck the flyer away and exit at Fifty-Ninth Street. Climbing the steps I catch sight of Christopher Columbus perched way up on his plinth, gazing southward over the snarl of traffic that is Eighth Avenue. His proud head, his floppy hat are etched against the clear sky. Among the morning throng of bicycle renters and newspaper sellers, there is a man clutching a large black Bible and crying out:

"*Jesus is coming. Prepare your heart. Get ready! Jesus is coming!*"

He has a stack of booklets. As with the screaming vegan, I can't resist. I reach for one to add to my collection of fliers, leaflets, fortunes, and pamphlets—ever on the hunt for a clue to the riddle. For instance, the last fortune I opened at a teashop in San Francisco:

An angry man has his mouth open, and his eyes shut.

I pause now to glance at my newest pamphlet. The title is in red.

Eternal Life Is a Free Gift!

The first line on the first page is printed in bold black ink:

Doing Good Works Can Not Save You!

And on the last page I find a passage that gives me pause.

"Where as you know not what shall be in the morrow. For, what is your life? It is even a vapour, that appeareth for a little time, and then vanisheth away." (James 4:14)

I step inside the huge hospital and take the elevator to the second floor. I wait by the door of the clinic near a wooden statue of Saint Luke, patron of doctors and painters. Siba is not there yet so I just hang out a bit with Luke. Then, I spot him coming down the hall. I just know it's him. Tall, ambling African in blue jeans and blue shirt.

I'd never have guessed his age. His gait is way adult but young, too, somehow. The report tells me: twenty-four. He keeps looking at a paper in his palm, and up at the numbers on the doors along the corridor. I lean out and wave. He walks right up and grabs my hand and he grins.

His smile startles me. I realize I was expecting someone broken.

I'M FORTY-TWO YEARS OLD; I HAVE A LITTLE TAPE RECORDER stashed in my pocket. A nurse at the front desk directs me to an elevator, the second floor. I walk the stark hall, rehearsing lines in my head, thinking I may go blank when I lay eyes on him. *Bob, do you recall when we last saw one another? How we met?* I feel the chatter in my head, the load of past strapped to my ribs.

I find him propped in a bed, poking at a piece of broccoli with a plastic fork. He looks like someone's grandmother: mop of hair, glasses. After a befuddling moment the face comes into focus. Under the puffed skin comes the rugged mug of the thirty-year-old pedophile, the mountain-climbing, flannel-wearing counselor. He has a roommate, a brown-skinned man, staring at a TV fixed high on the wall.

"Let's go outside," he says.

He wheels himself down the hall into a crowded elevator. I stand just behind him like a visiting nephew, a devoted son. Or that's what I believe the staff and patients crammed in with us might assume. How dear of the young to visit the old.

We find a spot under a palm tree and it is there that we converse. He is slumped in the shade, this mountainous myth in my head, reduced to a blob of human flesh sitting in a wheelchair, missing part of a foot. He speaks of his family and his frail health and I recount a slice of my life in Manhattan. Finally, I press the little button in my pocket as I press toward the point.

I remember leaning forward to clasp my hands as I tried to describe for him the endless fallout from his crime (which feels like *our* crime, which of course is the crime): my teenage suicide attempts, the monstrous sexual compulsions, the chaos. I am

52

direct and honest with him but my voice and words remain oddly
rational, restrained in a way that strikes me as far away. Lacking
flesh. And even as I speak in quiet, grown-up tones, somewhere
in a region far away and down deep, somewhere in a land of lions,
a hungry maw is growling.

OK, Martin, before you leave, let him have it.

Let the motherfucker have it!

At one point he says, "I hope you don't hate me."

And I don't know if it's the way his head is hanging in the sun,
or his puffy cheek, but something about him just . . . slays my
heart. It's as if in a flash I glimpse him as a kid, a hurt and struggling child. And the words tumble from my mouth:

"Look, Bob. Whatever else there might have been, there was
kindness, too, you were kind and I don't hate you."

And I, or *something*, ends up . . . my hand reaches out and
squeezes his shoulder.

Meeting done.

I turn and walk down the sunny sidewalk and drive away in
my rent-a-car.

Damn.

What in the world was that?

ONE NIGHT MY FRIEND, my longtime agent, Steve, comes to see the one-man play in which I recount the scene with Bob in the hospital—the moment when I squeeze his shoulder.

Steve is a great guy, a father of three. I love him. After the show in the theater lobby, he grabs me, takes me aside, and says,

"So, wait a minute. You had a tape recorder in your pocket when you went to confront that jerk?"

"Yeah."

"Jeez. I would have had a fucking gun."

His eyes tell me he is 100 percent serious. I'm stunned at the ferocity of his anger on my behalf. A heat fills my lungs, moves up my throat, and I take his hand in both of mine and squeeze, as if his palm is a trigger, his passion a warm bullet to the heart.

SOMETIMES, WHEN I THINK OF RAGE, I picture the face of the author-activist Larry Kramer, a man known for getting his dander up. I've watched him (several times) in a famous clip in which he explodes at an ACT UP meeting. This was caught on shaky, black-and-white film back in the early days of the AIDS epidemic. If you Google it, it comes up as:

"Larry Kramer's Epic 'Plague' Rant."

In the clip you can witness the meeting deteriorate into bickering and name-calling when, suddenly, Kramer erupts like Vesuvius. He screams at the top of his lungs,

"*Plague!*"

A thick moment of utter silence follows and then,

"We are in the middle of a fucking plague! . . . Until we get our act together, *all of us*, we are as good as dead!"

It's heart-stopping. Biblical.

I remember seeing Kramer on *Nightline*, mid-epidemic. He faces Ted Koppel and the huge TV audience with pure, articulate fury about the public and political indifference toward the AIDS crisis. Koppel falls uncharacteristically dumb. As do I. Silent in the face of such power and passion and, some say, lunacy. I am in awe of his anger. His voice is strangled, choking on the imperative to save fellow citizens. Dying citizens, who are not being embraced, heard, cared for by their government, their fellows. It is a desperate call to arms, to compassion. He seems the embodiment of a holy rage, the quintessence of ACT UP's famous slogan:

Silence = Death.

"WAS THIS FROM THE WOODEN CLUB OR was this from the broken glass?"

The doctor pointed to a scar on Siba's upper arm.

"Club," he answered.

I watched the doctor write on the clipboard as I translated. After several more questions, the soft-spoken doctor thanked Siba. He told us he was sure he had ample evidence for the report, that this was a strong case. He touched Siba's shoulder for a moment. "Good job, young man. And good luck." Siba struggled suddenly against a sob and, despite my attempt to disappear, be professional, I did, too.

Siba and I walked out of the clinic and down the hall and stepped outside. It was a bright day. The air and sunlight, after nearly three hours in the cramped room, were a great relief. We walked the long way around past Lincoln Center toward the subway station. We moved in silence until, like some nervous tour guide, I started pointing at buildings, addressing Siba in choppy, cheerful French, as if he were on holiday.

"That's the Met there, where they do opera and big theater things and that one, the one with all the glass? That's Alice Tully Hall—for music mostly. You know? Symphonies. And there, lots of dance over there—New York City Ballet and—"

"Ballet?" he said. "*La danse?*"

"*Oui.*"

He stopped and put his arms straight into the air, and let them fall slowly and then fly up again as he turned in a circle.

"*Oui, comme ça,*" I said.

We exchanged smiles and walked on.

I told him,

"That's what I do for work, can you believe?"

"*La danse?*"

"*Le théâtre, la danse, tout ça.*"

He nodded. We rounded the corner. I couldn't help it, I started pointing again.

"Look down there. That statue, on the tall pedestal? That's Christopher Columbus. He discovered America, sort of."

Siba nodded and then asked,

"Martin, *qu'est-ce que ça veut dire, opéra?*" What does opera mean?

"Um . . . big stories. *Les grandes histoires,* tales of love, betrayal, told with lots of singing."

He seemed perplexed. There was a hedge with a little wall in front of it. I jumped up, opened my arms, and belted out a few measures of Puccini. Siba looked completely stunned. Then, he doubled over and burst out laughing—a long and wonderful laugh.

When we got to the subway station we checked that he had enough for fare to New Jersey. He pulled a bill and coins from his pocket. We counted. He had just enough and I found myself digging in my jeans. I handed him a twenty. Wrong move. (Boundaries, the instructor had said.) He shook his head, refused. Then, shyly, accepted. It was awkward. It was as if I was underlining the distance: I'm in this club, this country club. He's not. I wrote my number on the page of a notebook, ripped it out, and handed it to him.

"Look, if you need anything."

He nodded. I stuttered, "I . . . I can't tell you how . . ." I stopped and stared at the gum-smacked floor. My chest bursting with I don't know what—the day, our meeting? Finally, I looked up and said, "I'm taking the blue, the A down to the theater, and you," I pointed to the orange circle, "*Vous prendrez ça, oui? Le D*, D three stops to Thirty-Fourth Street, then look for the PATH, right? PATH train."

"*Oui, merci.*"

He took my hand. His grip, his eyes, surprised me to tears, and we moved toward each other and embraced.

FORGIVENESS WAS A WORD the nuns often chalked on the board. I understood that it was crucial to who we were, *should* be. But, as far as I could tell, it was something deeply tricky, something that Jesus was up to but not the likes of me.

At first, the questions were simple.

"When do we forgive? Like, when someone steals from you?"

"Yes."

"When someone hits you?"

"Yes. That's a real test. When someone really hurts you. Will you find the grace to forgive or will you strike back?"

A girl raised her hand. I don't recall who or what grade. We were small and she, like all the girls in my class, wore a pleated skirt a dark shade of green. She raised her hand and asked what seemed the central question:

"But why, Sister . . . *why* do people hurt one another?"

Sister's voice became quiet, as if speaking to herself.

"When we are hurt, when we're in pain, we must think of it as an invitation guiding us toward His boundless Love. Think of this Earth as a school with difficult lessons. How but through the trials of the world can we come to know God?"

My classmate sat looking distinctly unsatisfied.

Years later, I came across a letter that a young Keats had written to his brother and sister. While reading it, I thought of the nuns, of my schoolmate's long-ago question. Keats begins his lengthy missive by telling his siblings about a black eye he received while playing cricket. Then, deep into the letter he writes:

> *The common cognomen of this world among the misguided and superstitious is "a vale of tears" from which we are to be redeemed by a certain arbitrary interposition of God and taken to Heaven. What a little circumscribed straightened notion! Call the world if you Please "The vale of Soul-Making." Then you will find the use of the world. . . .*
>
> *Do you not see how necessary a World of Pains and troubles is to school an Intelligence and make it a Soul? A Place where the heart must feel and suffer in a thousand diverse ways! Not merely is the Heart a Hornbook, It is the Minds Bible, it is the Minds experience, it is the teat from which the Mind or intelligence sucks its identity. As various as the Lives of Men are—so various become their Souls, and thus does God make individual beings, Souls, Identical Souls of the Sparks of his own essence.*

IT WAS THE SUMMER OF 2004 and I was in my hometown, Denver, performing a monthlong run of the one-man play. One night after the show, I stepped out into the parking lot and saw a bearded man standing there. It seemed he was waiting for me. A dark-haired woman was holding his arm. Something in his lanky stance, the upturned twist of his mouth, was familiar. He stepped toward me and tried to smile, he raised his hand, and it came in a flash—*Ben? My old camping buddy Ben?* I instantly recalled the braces on his teeth, his lighter hair, his loping gait—the Ben of fourteen, one of Bob's boys. His face snapped into focus across thirty years. In a flash I remembered how we chopped wood and set up tents and rafted the Green River. His jaw was trembling; there were tears all over his face and then his arms were around me, his head buried in my shoulder saying over and over,

"We made it, man. We made it."

We went and sat at the side of the parking lot with his wife, Cindy. He told me how he worked heavy machinery, showed me photos of their two kids perched on snowmobiles and their house in Evergreen, Colorado. And then he said, "Marty. I'm sick. I have AIDS, man."

"What?"

"Yeah. I just, I guess I couldn't erase what happened with . . . with Bob . . ." His words leaped out now as if long trapped. "I was thirteen, you know. He'd give me Budweiser, fuck me, and . . . I don't know, through the years it snuck up and took hold. I've got a wife, kids, for Christ's sake . . . but I would go find men. I never knew where my feet were taking me. I wanted to kill myself."

"I know, Ben. Been there."

"I know you have," he said. "Jesus, man. I can't believe you wrote all that down and made a story out of it. We could never say anything back then, could we? Even though we . . ." His voice trailed off.

He turned to his wife. "Cindy, she knows all this now."

She smiled a wan smile, took my hand, thanked me—all of it so much so fast, and Ben turned to me again and said,

"I found you. It's fate. Let's keep in touch, man. Let's keep in touch."

THE PHONE CALL CAME LATE one afternoon, as I was about to leave for the theater to strap on my *Spamalot* outfit. He introduced himself as Peter.

"I'm a playwright and actor and sometimes producer," he told me. His was a polite, British-sounding voice, slightly muffled in the buzz of what turned out to be long distance. He was calling from Africa. South Africa. He explained that his company was producing and he himself performing my one-man play. "We'd like you to come for a week or more to help us publicize the show. There will be a panel at the university: 'How Do You Forgive the Unforgivable?' We'd like you to be on it. We think the panel will generate interest in the play and its themes."

I wondered what he meant by themes. Did I have some in mind when I wrote the play?

"There will be theater artists and a government representative or two and some journalists speaking. It would be great if you could participate. My colleagues and I think it would be an exciting cultural exchange."

"Gosh, wow, Africa," is about all I managed to say.

He filled the silence.

"Have you ever heard about the Truth and Reconciliation Committee?"

"Kind of, yes. The hearings and so on . . . after apartheid?"

"You know the gist? The commission was set up to provide a space in which those who had been victims of human rights violations could make their stories heard, apply for investigations to be done, reparations to be given. Amnesty would be provided for those who had violated human rights if they were truthful, took responsibility. Restorative justice rather than retributive justice."

The words *restorative, retributive* rang in my head. So, there's more than one kind of justice? This struck me as wise, obvious, though I hadn't thought of it before. I expressed this to Peter and then I asked him what he meant by *themes* in the play.

"Well, the complexity of forgiveness, certainly. We think your play is provocative on a personal level that certainly speaks to the larger political sphere here. Regarding, I mean, the idea of pardon, of compassion."

"That's . . . well, gee, I see that," I mumbled, as I thought how odd it was to have become a kind of go-to guy on forgiveness.

"I think you'd like it here," he said.

"Oh. I'm sure I would. My God. Africa."

"Will you consider coming?"

"IT'S SIMPLE, ANGER IS DARWINIAN," an attorney friend said to me one day. "It exists to make you *effective*. Since the beginning, its function is survival."

"Seems you get angry a lot," I told him.

"Comes with the territory. I try to be reasonable but sometimes I just lose it. You know, I'm human."

"You're a lawyer."

"That, too."

"I'm so terrified of confrontation," I said. "I think I'm hung up on being 'good.' Do you ever," I asked him, "do you ever view anger as the opposite of compassion? I mean, that a burst of rage is basically a loss of awareness, an obliteration of empathy? A rash of unconsciousness that tears human souls asunder?"

"But what about anger that is *born* of compassion?" he posed. "An urgent fury, a demand for action. That's what's at the root of most good laws. Look at the anger it took and still takes to speak up for civil, for human rights. Anger can give you a moral lucidity."

"Yeah . . ."

"Look at Christ in the temple."

"I knew you were going to say that."

"I mean, he was a pretty empathetic guy. And from what I hear, he could get totally fucking pissed off."

MY FIRST GLIMPSE OF AFRICA CAME AT DAWN. Out the little oval window next to my seat on Delta flight 1249. I caught sight of the blinking lights and early-morning bustle of the Dakar airport. We'd just completed the first long leg of the trip over the Atlantic from Atlanta to Senegal. We were parked on the tarmac refueling. It was a warm September morning, 2007.

I crawled over the girl next to me, who had informed me upon buckling into her seat, just after boarding, that she was downing an Ambien. She'd pulled it from her knapsack rather theatrically, along with a Poland Spring water. "I plan to remain unconscious," she said, "until I walk into the arms of my boyfriend in Joburg. Don't worry about stepping over me. Don't worry about anything. Good night." She popped the pill, then gave me a grin before putting on her sleeping mask. That was an ocean ago, I thought, as I stepped over her body and into the aisle to stagger to the front of the plane for a pee.

I encountered a bright-awake man who was restocking food items and removing trash. He was part of the local ground crew. He was working quickly as I approached the toilet.

"*Bonjour,*" I said, assuming this was one of his tongues. He answered in a mellifluous French, saying, "Good day" and asking if my trip had been good so far. His face was vivid in contrast to the planeload of slumbering passengers. I had a vague idea of Senegal as enchanted, full of sun and music, and I paused to ask if he was from Dakar.

"*Oui,*" he replied.

"I hear it is beautiful."

"It is," he said. "You should stay longer." His grin was morning sun, white teeth rising from night.

"I'd like to," I replied.

"Yes," he said. "Don't skip Africa. This Africa." He nodded out the window toward his city.

A man clad in what looked like a hazmat suit suddenly made his way down the aisle, a contraption strapped to his back, the nozzle of a hose clutched in his hand. He looked like a beekeeper spraying his hives, a gardener dispensing a pesticide over the heads of sleeping plants. It was eerie. Apparently, we were being fumigated. Against what we carried or what we'd encounter, I had no clue.

The Senegalese man nodded a friendly good-bye as I stepped into the john and ducked away from the fumigator. We took off and spent the rest of the day flying south over a desert as vast as the ocean we'd crossed the night before.

I landed in a guesthouse in a quiet section of Johannesburg. The place was run by a chipper woman who'd grown up in neighboring Rhodesia, now called Zimbabwe. She spoke with great passion and nearly nonstop about the evils of Mugabe and his reign of terror. She explained that many of her staff were people who'd fled Zimbabwe. That she wanted to employ at least a few of the countless refugees who'd risked crossing the border into South Africa to seek work and send money back home to their desperate families. "They come from their troubled country and land here in South Africa, an entire nation suffering post-apartheid PTSD."

The guesthouse was tucked away in a green-filled corner of Joburg. The bungalows and palm trees here made for a bucolic oasis amid the jam-packed rush of this huge economic hub. The quiet little neighborhood actually reminded me of West Hollywood.

I had a few free days before I was to meet up with the theater troupe. I consulted my guidebook, which highlighted with a red star the not-to-be-missed sites: Soweto; the Apartheid Museum; Constitution Hill, where you can visit Gandhi's prison cell. Wait. *Gandhi's* prison cell? What was *he* doing here?

Tommy, the driver I'd hired, took me there. I found the exhibit about Gandhi. It was like entering a sanctified space. My body tingled at beholding artifacts, evidence of his presence. There were recordings of his voice, photographs and texts about him on the wall near his former prison cell. I learned that he was working in South Africa as a young lawyer. This was in the late 1800s. He had only recently finished his law studies in England. As an Indian, a brown-skinned man, he experienced violent discrimination in South Africa, which spurred him to organize on behalf of the horribly exploited Indian laborers working in the many mines of Johannesburg and beyond. This was where Gandhi first began honing his revolutionary tactic of nonviolent protest, which is often called "passive resistance." I found a book about this and read a few passages:

". . . as the struggle advanced, Gandhi found the name 'passive resistance' inadequate to express its real meaning, since it was being looked upon as a 'weapon of the weak.'"

Someone came up with *sadagraha* or "firmness in a good cause." Gandhi then adopted a slightly different word:

satyagraha: truth (*satya*) implies love, and firmness (*agraha*) engenders and therefore serves as a synonym for force.

Gandhi wrote:

"I thus began to call the Indian movement 'Satyagraha,' that is to say: The Force that is born of Truth and Love or non-violence."

You can walk through his dank and tiny cell, past the toilets that he was ordered to scrub. Later, I found more texts of Gandhi's in a museum shop devoted to his life and work.

. . . I believe that non-violence is infinitely superior to violence, forgiveness is more manly than punishment.

Forgiveness is the quality of the brave, not of the cowardly.

I have learnt through bitter experience the one supreme lesson to conserve my anger, and as heat conserved is transmuted into energy, even so our anger controlled can be transmuted into a power which can move the world.

It is not that I do not get angry. . . . I only control my anger when it comes. How I find it possible to control it would be a useless question, for it is a habit that everyone must cultivate and must succeed in forming by constant practice.

I DROVE WEST TOWARD THE MOUNTAINS TO BEN'S PLACE. Cindy made a late lunch. I met their two kids. Fine-boned and blond like their dad. A polite girl about ten years old, a shy boy of twelve. I felt a familiar tremor as I took in the boy's small frame, his slight hand clasping mine. Twelve. That was Ben and me a blink ago.

After we all ate, Ben and I sat alone on his back porch nursing beers. Two snowmobiles were parked next to the porch. They were each encased in dark-blue plastic covers. The foothills of the Front Range rose just beyond his backyard. He'd made a sweet home, I thought.

"Cindy," he said, after a swallow of beer, "she saved me, you know. Thank God I met her. At a Broncos game, when I was at my lowest."

He told me a story.

"When I was like, eighteen, nineteen, my dad basically kicked me out of the house. I was drinking—not as much as *he* was—but I was going down. Done with school or it was done with me and I couldn't seem to find or hold a job. I didn't know where I was going. Bob had always said, you know, 'Get in touch if you need anything.'

"He'd moved out to California by then. I think he had to leave Colorado cause of legal shit? Anyway, I had his info. It's crazy, I know, but it's like I blocked out the bad and remembered the ways he always tried to help. 'Cause he did. Man, he taught me carpentry, he taught me tools, woodwork. Did you see our kitchen shelves inside? I built them. Bob taught me how to do that. He taught me a lot—a lot of useful things. Shit."

Ben turned to me, shrugged.

"Anyway, I guess I was still, you know, I still thought of him as a kind of a friend. A fucked-up friend but . . . I don't know. He paid attention to me and . . . you know . . . I called."

Ben winced, took a gulp, kept talking.

"It was this little town. He had an OK place. Small. Cars and trucks around that he worked on. I would do odd jobs for him. I had a place to sleep but it was . . . it was bad. I guess I was too old now to be of any real interest to him. We argued about everything. I drank. He bitched. You remember he had a temper? He could be a total asshole. I just got angrier and angrier and, you know, there were boys hanging around. Neighborhood kids. Some Mexicans. Things were happening, I think. I could feel it. You know. And he treated me like shit and I hated him, hated being there. You remember how he always had a gun around. That thirty aught six?"

I nodded. "Sure do."

"Well, I got to thinking. Maybe that's why I came. To . . . to kill him."

Ben smiled, looked off toward the mountains.

"I found his gun one night, hidden away in a drawer, can you believe? I took the gun and I stood there and thought about pointing it at Bob's sleeping head. I wanted that motherfucker dead. Dead. I guess I was just realizing, remembering all that had gone down when I was thirteen, fourteen, and I was pointing the gun and standing there and . . . I could see the freakin' headlines! *Abuse victim shoots molester in fit of rage!* Or some shit like that and it hit me and all I could think was: '*Don't* ruin your life. Don't make Bob the bigger victim.' I would be the one going to jail for what he started, what he had done. Then he'd *win*. I didn't want him to win. I didn't. I left. That's the last I saw of him. One day, not long after, I was at a Denver Broncos football game, cold as hell day and . . . I met Cindy. Thank God. I met Cindy. She saved me."

Ben and I sat on the picnic table in his backyard for a long while, dusk falling. Then he said,

"You know, I told my kids it's leukemia. They don't know what's happening, why I'm so pale and skinny. I can see they're scared. Shit, I'm scared."

Then he smiled, still the white teeth, the blond hair, the rugged looks of a western ranch boy.

His kids came outside and asked if they could go across the street and play at a friend's house.

"Be back soon. Mom made ice cream."

His two beloveds nodded and said something along the lines of nice to meet you.

"Great kids," I said as they darted off.

Ben nodded as he watched them go, his grin cracking his face, lighting his eyes. We sipped our beers.

I saw the words written on a pamphlet in the lobby of the guesthouse. Like a five-word poem, a summons, it called to me. It was a starred site. I leafed through the pages. The photos of fossils and caves and the drawings of prehistoric humanoids stirred me bone deep. Ever since I was a kid I've loved anthropology, the buried marrow, the missing links.

I'd heard about this place but had no idea it was here, so close to Johannesburg. When Tommy came to fetch me that morning I showed him the flyer, saying, "I've got to go! Is it far?" Tommy, a quiet gentleman with darkest skin, missing a front tooth, shook his head and said it wasn't too long a drive, about fifty kilometers. So, off we went past wild olive and stinkwood trees, to this World Heritage Site, tucked amid the hills of southern Africa.

When we arrived we met our guide, Ruben, a young man wearing a white baseball cap. Ruben greeted our little group of seven or eight tourists. Swinging his arm across the vast grassland, he said,

"Welcome. This is the place where humans first mastered fire."

He brought both his hands together, fingertips and thumbs barely touching, as if cradling a butterfly. "Welcome to this site where more than 40 percent of all our human ancestor fossils have been uncovered." A tingle ascended my spine.

We followed Ruben toward a small museum. I had been asking Tommy about the many tribes and languages of South Africa (eleven official and dozens of tribal tongues), and as we walked Tommy told me that, like him, Ruben was Zulu. "I can tell by his face, cheekbones; his dialect. The woman who sold us the tickets," he said, "the one with the long dress? She's Xhosa."

Once inside the museum, Ruben led us past a fabulously lit display of our relatives. Not just any skull 'n' bones but the world-famous Little Foot. They had most of his frame and his whole gnarly foot on a platter. And right nearby the head of three-million-year-old Mrs. Ples propped up beneath a spotlight. Fragments of people discovered right here, out of the limestone and into the limelight. Celebrity skeletons!

We passed several dioramas. A furry family of Neanderthals was posed as if crouching near a fire. Neanderthals, the ancestral line that mysteriously ceased to be, beat out, most likely, by the more aggressive and clever *Homo sapiens*. We passed three-dimensional figures of *Australopithecus*, *Homo habilis*, *Homo erectus*. Then Ruben led us outside past a pit where several hominids from the nearby anthropology school were at work, kneeling in the dirt, dusting up old secrets.

We walked along a footpath and stopped not far from the mouth of the Sterkfontein Cave—a huge fissure chock-full of our kins' buried bones. And here, embedded in stone like the Holy Grail, was a shiny plaque. Ruben said,

"Before we climb down into the cave, take a moment to study this."

So, our little group—Tommy and me, a tall, shimmering couple from Switzerland, their two towheaded kids, a young Japanese pair, and three older Australian ladies with tote bags—we all gazed at this bronze etching. It was a map, a depiction of Earth with all seven continents fitted together. And Ruben asked,

"Have any of you ever heard the term 'Pangaea?' It's from the Greek, meaning 'One Earth.' It is the theory that there was an

ancient super continent that began fracturing, splitting apart—
tectonic accidents, violent shifts—two hundred million years or
so ago. Some say that, like our galaxies, our continents are drifting back together. As you've drifted here today. Here, all the lands
of the world are reunited."

We stared at the amazing jigsaw. I noticed that the coasts of
Senegal and South Carolina were spooning. Ruben said,

"We know that earliest humans began right here and mi-
grated all across the globe—black to brown to white. So," he
lowered his voice, "so, I may as well say to all of you . . ." He gave
us a dazzling grin.

"I may as well say . . . *welcome home.*"

HOW DO WE MEASURE THE DEPTH, the breadth of an injustice? Determine the extent of damage done, damages to be paid? This is what we ask of our legislators and our courts of law. To define and measure crimes, weigh the punishments.

"Colorado Sex Offenses: Sexual Assault on a Child" is one of the many numbing texts I have thumbed through. There are countless statutes that attempt to make math out of the murk of trespass. I can't stand to read too much or too closely. Can't stand to think of myself as victim. It's astonishing to glance at the endless graphs and pages, the categories and subsections, to think of the numberless stories that gave rise to these numbered laws, to think of the many men and women who sat in august chambers to ponder the dark tales that demanded the creation of these decrees in the first place.

From what I can glean, Ben and I experienced a Class 4 felony. Certain questions attempt to pin things down.

How long did the abuse go on?

What was the age difference between victim and perpetrator?

How many times did the act occur?

Was there penetration?

Oh that word, *penetration*. It gives pause. It penetrates. A stab to the gut even as I mark a certain wave of relief (a stubborn point of pride?) rising up as I think, well, at least I held on to my virginity. (Blessed Virgin). Even now convincing myself that I was then and am now *less* a victim because he didn't "enter" me. Besides blowing me, what Bob mainly engaged in, engaged me in, I have since learned is called "intercrural intercourse" or "interfemoral sex." Also known in some circles as "the Ivy League rub." It means, essentially, placing the penis between the legs, the thighs. Less shame in that, right? That he came between my legs, less harm to sensitive tissue, to delicate manhood. I realize in this moment of writing that this is how I've always thought of it. What happened to me was not quite so bad, not *actually* rape, you see.

But of course, I've come to know just how deeply he penetrated my life. How he fucked with innocence. I understand now, more than ever, how in his act of molestation I took on *being evil.* I chose to *allow* it to happen. Or so I deeply (so deep it remained hidden in me) believed. And so began an insistent self-directed rage.

We might, in the wake of becoming a victim, ask ourselves:

How much "self" was lost or *found* as a result of this wrongdoing? Am I ruined? Am I stronger?

Has this very hurt, this crucifixation, become a lifelong guide, my shaman of dark and light pointing the way toward liberation? Can I one day let it all just go? Am I simply a sum of all these things and people that have happened? It all happened, therefore, *I* happened. Just as I am. No regrets.

We tend to look toward others to compare, to weigh our narratives, don't we? Our fortunes and misfortunes? What's your story? Am I more damaged than you? Luckier?

We may well ask all these things if we are still alive, that is, to do the asking. Whatever the thoughts, whatever the measuring, here I am growing older and Ben is not.

It was seven months after that night we found each other in the parking lot of the Curious Theatre in Denver, Colorado, that his wife called to tell me that Ben had dropped dead at work.

"A stroke," she said. "He couldn't fight it anymore."

"I'm so sorry," I said, hanging up the phone, breathing crazy, thinking of all the ways that that monster had murdered lanky Ben thirty years ago. And I see it then, I still do. Standing there, a pistol in my palm. Bob's head, the pasty priests who hired him, shattering like pumpkins.

Justice.

ONE NIGHT, I STAYED AT A FANCY LODGE on the outskirts of Johannesburg. I had inquired about a place where I might find some "natural Africa," some countryside, a respite from the big city. Being short on time I settled for a place a tour agent had told me about not more than a two-hour drive from the center of town. "A lodge by a river, tucked away in the hills," she'd said. "It caters to fishermen, I think, but it is supposed to be lovely and there are some wild animals about and a few hiking trails." I asked Tommy to drop me there late one afternoon; he planned to retrieve me late the following day to head back to the city.

My room was ridiculously large and full of amenities—slippers and robes and a hot tub and a patio overlooking the low, dry hills and the man-made pond. There was a fireplace and a bottle of wine. The largeness and plushness, in contrast to the townships and crushing crowds of laborers we'd seen packed in trucks traveling along the highway, made me feel a wasteful and oh-so-American tourist. I ordered ostrich for dinner in the opulent dining room. It was delicious, but I chewed it self-consciously, eyeing the many white South African men who appeared to be regulars here. I caught snatches of conversation about fishing and golf and hunting.

I got up very early and walked for an hour or so along the trails. I spotted a single giraffe, standing alone. Plucked from somewhere and dropped here, it seemed, as ambience. He was nibbling at a scrawny-looking leaf hanging from a scrawny-looking tree stuck on a hill of dry, yellow grass. It seemed it was his job to say, "Africa." But as I climbed farther I saw a small herd of eland, magical creatures. Their shape—elk-like with the sharp angles of antelopes—their serene stance, put me in mind of ancient cave paintings.

I headed back down the slope to the lodge thinking I'd try to write down a few thoughts about the trip before breakfast. A small gravel path curved downward and dropped me at the back of the main lodge. Two staff members in the maroon uniforms worn by all who worked there, a young woman about thirty and a younger man, mid-twenties, I'd say, were chatting quietly. It appeared that they were on a break from their duties. I gave a little wave as I passed. They nodded, smiled.

I remembered the woman. Tommy had stopped to pick her up on the road the evening before. She had been walking up the long and steep road that led to the entrance of the lodge. When he came up beside her, he stopped the van. "A ride, Sister?" (Tommy had a way of greeting practically everyone we came across. He'd say, "Sister," if it was a woman and, for a man, "Yo Bah," with a friendly wave of his hand. I asked him what that meant. "Short for 'Yo Boss,'" he told me.) The young woman accepted the offer of a ride and the two of them slipped into a native tongue. She looked at me once, shyly, as we drove. When she got out of the van I asked Tommy if they were speaking Zulu. "No, Sotho," he said. "In this part of the Transvaal, Sotho is common."

I paused now on the path and said, "Good morning. We gave you a ride last night, remember? I mean, the driver I was with, stopped to give you a ride."

She nodded. She was so beautiful—a clear and incandescent smile, the glow of her skin. The man was silent and striking. I walked on then I heard the young woman ask,

"Where are you from?"

"United States. New York."

"Oh, man!" said the guy, now grinning. "Michael Jackson!"

"Are you traveling alone?" She asked.

"Yep."

A pause, she smiled.

"Where's your wife?"

In my short time here, I had already been asked this a few times. It startled me at first. But I began to realize that a person traveling all alone was an oddity here.

One instance of this was most memorable.

I had called for a taxi one evening. A man arrived. I got in.

"Traveling alone?" he asked.

"Yes," I replied.

"Do you have a wife?"

"No, I don't."

"No kids?"

"No."

"You?" I asked.

"Of course. Four children. Three sons."

We were quiet for a time. I don't quite remember how it came up, but he asked more questions, and I finally just said that I had a partner, that I lived with a man. What I do recall distinctly was what he said next.

"I knew the moment I saw you."

"Knew what?"

"That you're that way."

"Really?"

"Yeah. Hey, it's cool." He paused, then continued. "God does not accept you. I think you will all go to hell, but you are very nice people and you're really good for business. You use the cabs a lot. I appreciate it."

He said all this in a very matter-of-fact way. It wasn't belligerent. It was just . . . shocking. The rest of the trip we remained silent. I considered not tipping. But in the end, I did. Very little.

The young woman's face was open and bright and I said,

"I . . . I don't have a wife."

"No children?"

"No."

"Oh, no children?" she said. She seemed then to be calculating something—the depth of my loss, the end of my bloodline? I glanced at the man, who was just then making a half-hearted attempt to wipe the morning dew from a table. I took the plunge. Why at this late date in life it still feels like a plunge is, God knows, a complex question, but I recognize an abiding vulnerability in revealing my sexuality. Especially in a foreign land with customs I don't understand. Though, in this case, a country with a constitution containing the most progressive human rights protections on the planet, including explicit GLBT protections. Still, there it was, the sting of my own homophobia, a stab of danger as I said,

"I live with a man. We've been together many years."

She looked at me, nodded slightly.

The man stopped wiping. He looked at me.

"Yeah, man. OK," he said.

There's a charge in the air. A sudden intimacy?

Then the man said: "It's good. If you hide, you suffer. Good to be who you are."

"Oh, yes," she agreed.

"Some are organizing in groups to fight for their rights. In the tribes," he said.

"Are there a lot of homosexuals in your tribe?" I asked.

"There aren't that many, no," he said.

She laughed then and said, "Oh, yes, oh, yes: many. But they hide it." He seemed not to mind that she contradicted him.

She told me her name was Edith. That she was Sotho. He called himself Alex. Zulu. I made a point of shaking their hands. I walked away toward the main hall and before I rounded the corner, I turned. They were watching me and smiling. I gave a small wave and then looked beyond them toward the hill, where the lone giraffe was grazing.

WE ARE SITTING ON BLUE COUCHES high above East Eighty-Sixth Street. The psychologist has welcomed us briskly, professionally and, clipboard in hand now, she dives right in to Siba's second required medical interview.

"Let me explain. I have a series of questions grouped in three basic categories, OK?"

Siba nods. "*Oui.*"

"First, I need to hear about your childhood, your family, your life growing up. Second, I'll need you to tell me about your arrest and torture in as much detail as you can. And lastly, we'll examine what you feel are the consequences of what happened to you."

When I finish translating this, Siba looks over to me, his brow furrowed.

"*Les conséquences,*" I repeat. He looks bewildered. I attempt to make the word clear. He shakes his head. I flounder, nervous, failing. How to clarify? I say something like, "It's the 'what happens' because of 'what happened'?" His face remains clouded; I search for other words. "*Les results après les événements de de de . . .*"

She's an older and quite proper lady, gray hair neatly coiffed. She wears glasses that are attached to a silver chain. The chain is strung with a series of small, pearl-like pebbles. It reminds me of my grandmother's rosary, which was laced with white beads, sets of ten, each decade comprising prayers devoted to the contemplation of mystery—the Sorrowful Mysteries, the Joyful, the Glorious. My grandmother knelt in her den to say her rosary each evening. I came upon her there a time or two, her white hair in a perfect drift so like this doctor who now perches her spectacles mid-nose to study her notes. Each time she addresses Siba, she lets them drop, and they dangle over her chest. Her face is solemn, all business. She gestures my way, indicating that we should move on from this snarl over the meaning of *consequences*. She continues down her list of questions, glasses rising then falling, pen scribbling. How many siblings? How much schooling? He moves through his history in one language, I repeat it in another. (How many times, I wonder, for how many officials will he rehearse his story?) New details emerge in this telling: his parents' difficult and distant marriage, his father's absence, the age of his siblings, daily life in a remote village, his marriage, his move to a big city. Years cross his face and then tears as he recounts the events of the day of his sudden arrest and torture. She asks again what he thinks is the *fallout* from his trauma.

He looks at me, the idea of trauma, I gather, and its half-life not computing. (I think of the *years*, the digging I've done.) I'm not sure if it's the divide of language, of culture, or simply what may be the absurdity or enormity of the question that has Siba stymied. He remains quiet and I wonder if this is just too abstract, if this narrative of cause and effect is too simple, too American. He stares past a large bookcase to a window where the Chrysler Building rises in the distance beyond countless Manhattan roofs and water tanks. I fumble again with the question, offering up words like *results* or *aftermath*, hoping one will make sense to him. I see what she's after, I know she needs the concrete in her report, but in this moment the query feels maladroit. We're stuck in silence.

She sets down her pen.

"OK, for instance," she says, "are you frightened when you hear loud noises?"

He remains silent.

"Is it hard to concentrate? Do you have trouble sleeping?"

He nods, and then he mentions persistent headaches. She scribbles—a measurement, a psychological mark, for the judge to read. Her pen poised again, she asks,

"Tell me, how is your life different now?"

He's sitting in a shrink's office on the Upper East Side of Manhattan staring out the window, rubbing his eyes. Everything's different, is it not?

She asks a few more things about his physical health, makes some notes, suggests that they get a doctor to examine him, to see about his headaches, then she looks up and says,

"I will write the best report I can for you. You are a brave young man. The United States would be lucky to have you."

Suddenly, he covers his face, chokes on the word "*merci.*" He crumples forward, reaches for Kleenex on the coffee table, and speaks in a rush now about his family, who are in hiding back in Sudan or Chad. "I . . . I hope," he says, "I hope I can bring them here one day. This is my dream. My dream." He presses the Kleenex to his eyes, trying to stop the flood of tears. After a moment the doctor turns to me and points to her watch.

I hustle Siba out of the room. He stops and leans against the hallway wall. "*Où se trouve la douche?*" he whispers. "*Où se trouve la douche?*" "Where is the shower?" He must mean the men's room. I find a key; he stays in there for a long time and then all the way down the elevator, out through the lobby, he can't stop crying. We step into the midday glare and walk west on East Eighty-Sixth Street. The lunch crowd weaves around us. Siba's chest is heaving, tears down his cheeks.

"Breathe, Siba. *Respire*," I say and for a moment I raise my right hand and press it against his back, between his shoulder blades. I dig into my jacket pocket, come up with a crumpled napkin. He takes it, wipes his eyes. We keep moving and when we get close to the corner of Park Avenue, he suddenly stops, looks down, and says,

"*Si je n'arrête pas . . .*" He shakes his head. "*Si je n'arrête pas de pleurer, je deviens aveugle.*" "If I don't stop crying, I will go blind."

"Tears are OK, helpful. Tears are . . ."

What to say?

We cross Park Ave. I can't just deposit him at the PATH station for his trip back to New Jersey, as instructed, so we just walk. He's got a slim windbreaker, no hat, no gloves. It's February! Freezing. Winter, like most things here, is a surprise for him.

"Hey, you want to maybe get some lunch or . . . ?"

He shakes his head, "No, *merci*."

But we cross Eighty-Sixth Street and end up sitting at the bar of a neighborhood restaurant, Demarchelier. Siba sips orange juice. I eat a bowl of leek soup. Above the shelves of liquor CNN is droning, scenes of Hillary versus Obama. Siba is transfixed by the program. It seems to calm him as he concentrates on the words. He's told me that this is how he is learning most of his English—by listening to American television. A map of the United States appears on the screen. I tell him I will get him a big one that he can put on the wall at home so that he and his housemates can study it. He nods. Silence. I ask him about his house in the city where he lived and about his family's village. He begins, tentatively, to describe his boyhood home. The land, the long days of sun. He tells me how his father was gone most of the time but was a good man. "There was a night . . ." he says. "I remember once, I had not seen my father for a long time, but suddenly he came into our sleep room very late and he woke my brother and me and fed us fresh goat milk. Right there in bed. It was still warm. 'Drink it *now*,' my father said. He wanted to see me get strong."

His eyes well up again. He stares past all the liquor bottles.

He begins to talk about his escape from prison. He tells me how he had no idea where he was. How the guards had taunted that he'd soon be shot. Meanwhile he was ordered to scour toilets, launder uniforms. One afternoon he was in the prison yard scrubbing shirts at a sink when he noticed they weren't looking at all. "They were all just talking, laughing about something. That's when I dove."

He explains how he jumped into a large drainage pipe that spilled into the nearby river. He swam downstream and met a man who understood his tribal tongue and then hid for months until a friend finagled a student visa. He landed at JFK on Christmas night. His first and only time flying. His friend had arranged for his travel that specific night, thinking it safer, that his departure would be less noticed. And things went smoothly for him at JFK where, for so many, it doesn't. If refugees enter without a valid visa, they're detained at the airport. Often handcuffed, they are interrogated and then either deported or put in a detention center, where they must pursue their asylum claim from within jail. Usually without the help of outside professionals.

Siba was lucky. He describes to me how he wandered JFK in search of his one brown bag.

"Martin," he says, "finally I found it, all by itself, going round and round this . . . thing."

He tells how he kept glancing at the "big glass wall" beyond which he could see traffic, people.

"I wondered how they got out there. I couldn't see any door. Finally, I walked up to get a closer look, leaned in and—whoosh— the wall of glass opened! *America*. So cold!"

The first person he spoke to was a taxi driver—from Mali, it turned out, a fellow Muslim. "I saw him standing next to his cab in a line of taxi cars. I knew he was a brother. A brother knows a brother's story without even asking. He offered me a bed in Brooklyn, and three days later, he dropped me in Jersey City. Lots of Sudanese, Chadians there so a chance of finding something, someone."

He goes quiet, staring numbly at his juice. We sit for a while. The place is nearly empty, CNN chattering softly above the shelves of liquor. There are two ladies sitting in the window, talking quietly over their white wine. Suddenly, Siba's arm shoots across my chest. He points to the two ladies, to the white curtains framing them. His face brightens.

"Martin, that's what I did at home!" he tells me. "When I moved to the city. I made curtains for people's houses."

He asks the barman for a pen. "*Un stylo?*" He grabs some napkins and starts drawing picture after picture of windows and drapes, the various ways they billow and hang. I ask him if I can keep one, if he will sign it for me. He laughs and signs with a great flourish—three names chock-full of vowels. He hands it to me, this guy with no job, who now lives in a tiny house with six other refugees. He hands the napkin to me, beaming.

"Martin," he says, "I will do this work again someday. In America."

His grin is wild. He punches me in the arm and his laugh bursts forth and I so want to know, I want to ask, how on earth is this possible, these shining eyes, after all that's happened?

I mean, where is his anger?

AFTER SIBA CAUGHT HIS PATH TRAIN that afternoon, I went for a swim at the West Side YMCA. I've belonged there for years, finding laps in the pool a fairly effective antidepressant. With hair still damp and endorphins rocking, I walked west up Broadway, the street and sidewalks packed with traffic. I approached the corner of Sixty-Sixth Street, aka "Peter Jennings Way." It's since turning fifty that I've noticed this: lively intersections named for the dead, all over town. I stopped at the curb to wait for the light, just across from a large white Mormon temple, its steeple topped with the Angel Moroni blowing his golden trumpet over the tangle of West Side traffic.

As I waited at the curb, I watched as an enormous SUV inched its way into the crosswalk just in front of me. It was one of those Humvee sorts of SUVs and I could see, just beyond the tinted glass, the frizzy head of a woman all alone, chatting on her cellphone. It was clear that she was eager to scoot onto Broadway before the light went against her. Traffic was snarled and she was braking and lurching and, you know, *late late late!*

Now, on the opposite corner of Peter's Place, stood a handsome woman in a white knit sweater who, the second the little stick figure signaled *Go*, stepped into the crosswalk. Meanwhile, the lady in the ten-passenger maxi tank was still determined, it seemed, to make her dash, to ignore the sweater-clad pedestrian until finally, she *honked*. A big Humvee honk. And that was it. The lady in the knit sweater turned, aimed her chest right at the hood of the Humvee, and hollered at the top of her lungs,

"Get your fucking gas guzzler out of my face! You are the reason we are in *Iraq*, bitch!"

Everything, it seemed to me, on that busy avenue in the shadow of the Mormon temple of Latter-day Saints, came to a standstill. Shock and Awe.

I mean, *nice* is OK, right? But let's admit it—

Anger is *awesome.*

It's one of the seven deadly sins. It's the first word in the first line of the freakin' *Iliad*:

Anger be now your song, immortal one. . . .

Anger gets things done in the world! Right?

But Seneca said rage is a spear with two points, one aimed toward the wielder. Aristotle said anger is *essential* for overcoming threats, a vital catharsis. In Buddhist tradition anger is called an addiction, or *visha*, a poison. Now that woman in the street, I stood there thinking, she's full of poison.

And I want to drink some of that.

Actually, I thought, I *need* to drink some of that.

Not two weeks later, I was back on Broadway, having just put in my thirty minutes crawling through the pool. It was another sunny day. I approached Sixty-Fifth Street, Leonard Bernstein Place, a block from Peter Jennings's, just steps from the Mormon temple.

The little man signaled *Go* and I moved briskly. I was halfway across the street when a cab, turning left off Columbus Avenue, barreled toward the crosswalk. I sensed his approach but held my course. He wouldn't dare breach the border, the white line protecting the vulnerable. But he kept moving. As if I did not exist, did not matter. Or, perhaps, he simply didn't see me? In any event, he was a few feet away when a roar erupted. Shockingly, mine. Like fire out my throat.

"HEY! I am WALKING HERE!"

I had a shoulder bag and in a flash I lifted it so that I could smash it against the hood of the cab, put a dent there. But at the very last second a dim remembrance that the bag held my Mac PowerBook (with its endless notes on compassion) stopped me. The cabby screeched to a halt. I got to the curb and turned and screamed, just *screamed*,

"This is a fucking crosswalk, man!"

The driver stuck his head out the window and said, "Fuck you."

"Yeah, well fuck you, too, you motherfucker!!!"

And we fell into each other's gazes for some eternal seconds— like two hungry beasts on the Serengeti. And, oh Lord, I took in his brown skin, long beard, his turban. A Sikh? A Muslim? His eyes were bloodshot (a rough day?). Whatever. I wanted to *win*. I wanted to scream something moral, like I'd seen the lady in the knit sweater do.

"You, you're the reason . . . the reason we're in Iraq!"

But that was so not right.

I got as far as—

"You! *You* . . . you're the *reason* . . ." But he was gone.

I looked around the sunny sidewalk to see if anyone had noticed the guy (me!) who *roared* like a lion. But, no, apparently, just another day on Lenny's corner. I walked, heart hammering, thinking I wanted to call my old therapist (one of them) and talk about this force, this *fury*. It *is* there, inside me. At least I'd located, unleashed it. Right? Something close to the real thing? At least this was not the thirty-year delayed reaction but—sword and shield, right in the moment, showing up to protect the innocent. If only I'd known this power way back when I was a kid, had punched Bob in the face, life would be different. Right? No victim, or *failure*.

I noticed a bus lumbering up Broadway with a huge poster plastered on its side, an ad for a big new movie:

Righteous Kill.

And there were De Niro and Pacino, all suited up, all barrels loaded. A caption just beneath the title said,

"*There's nothing wrong with a little shooting as long as the right people get shot!*"

And I thought, "Yeah, that's right, you guys, you big guns. Go get 'em! I get it. I'm not *soft*. I'm *hard. I'm in that fucking movie!*"

My heart was pounding. I spun around and sat on the edge of one of the Mormons' big potted planters, sat to catch my breath, until a nice man in uniform, guarding the house of Jesus Christ of Latter-day Saints, came and shooed me away. And told me, not unkindly, that this was no place for resting.

I WAS BACK IN DENVER FOR A VISIT and a dear high school friend invited me over for breakfast. Somewhere during the meal she asked,

"Have you seen *The Reader?*"

"Oh, I did," I replied. "I liked the film as much as the book. Kate Winslet did a terrific job playing that woman Hanna, don't you think?"

(Winslet played the central role of a Nazi prison guard who was brought to trial and punished, imprisoned, after the war.)

"What an *awful* character," my friend said. "Cold, chilling."

"I felt for her," I said. "You know, considering the horrible, complicated circumstances."

Then, very matter-of-fact, my friend said,

"Well, what she did was an evil past forgiveness. She forfeited her right to be called a human being."

This stopped me mid-chew. The *certainty* in her gaze was so Old Testament, very Dick Cheney. Her words shocked me even as I realized I found an odd comfort in my friend's steely power. She was utterly sure, in charge. The kind of in charge I imagine I would like to be.

"But sweetie," I said, "that guard was still a human being."

"Nope," she said, "that's not *human*."

"But it *is*. We do these things. They happen. We can't take humanity away from another person."

"She took it away by her actions. She allowed all those people she was guarding to die in that fire! She could have saved them just by unlocking the doors. There was no one there to stop her. She chose to put her supposed duty above her compassion. That was not human."

"But how can *we* make that judgment?" I asked.

"Not only can we, we *must*. We must have justice. Or we're lost."

Lost.

That word rang like a bell in my body. *Lost*, must be what I am. Doubt is all I feel sure of.

I often find myself saying:

"Oh, he was *so human*." And when I say it, I am referring to Bishop Tutu, Mandela, Gandhi. "She is a true human being, that Mother Teresa."

But might we just as accurately say this about Hitler or Stalin or the warlord Charles Taylor? Might we not say, Oh, he was *so human*.

AMONG THE MANY LOVELY MUSEUMS in San Diego's luscious Balboa Park, there's one called the Museum of Man. I'd been pedaling by it daily on my way to work at the Old Globe Theater, where I was employed in a short run of a popular comedy by the playwright Christopher Durang. It was 2014, the month was May, and it was busting out all over. Southern California showing off its every brilliant color. But each time I rounded one particular corner in the flower-filled park, right before I got to the theater, I'd see the large banner naming the current exhibit at the museum and my stomach would clutch, as if slamming a door on a blot of ugliness.

In hues of red and black it announced:

The History of Torture.

Each time I passed, I meant *not* to look at the sign but without fail, my attention was drawn there. My body repulsed and titillated all at once.

Now that's a hard sell, I thought. *Torture.* Won't be paying admission and ducking into that show anytime soon. Not on a sunny day anyway and, well, *every* day here is blessedly sunny.

One evening on my way out of the theater I happened to overhear a theatergoer talking about the "Torture" exhibit. About how truly unexpected and surprising it was. How *important.* "It tells us about ourselves," I heard her say, and a little bell went off in my head.

I showed up on a Friday afternoon, one of my last few days in San Diego. There was a ticket taker out front, an older docent with a tag that said "Betty" and a smile that said ready. "You're the actor, aren't you, playing at the Globe?" she asked.

"You have a good memory," I told her.

She remembered me not because of the play but because I had stopped by on my bike a week or so before to ask about the hours and the price of the exhibit. I'd mentioned I was working at the theater and, ever budget conscious, inquired about a possible employee discount.

"I'm sorry, there are no reduced rates for this special exhibit," she'd told me.

"Thanks," I'd said as I rode away feeling off the hook. Thinking I'd skip it after all. Fifteen dollars! I didn't want to pay *that* much for torture.

"Do come back," she sang out.

And several days later, I did.

"How's the play going?" she asked.

"Pretty well," I said. "It's selling. People seem to like it."

"I hear it's very funny."

"It is, I have to say."

I pulled out my wallet and she reached out to stop me.

"Put that away. Go on in," she said. Then whispered, "Don't tell on me."

"Hey. Thanks a lot."

Her white hair and yellow shirt shimmered as she waved me in. "Enjoy now."

A quote by Dostoyevsky greets you at the entrance.

Nothing is easier than to denounce the evildoer; nothing is more difficult than to understand him.

There's a brief description of what awaits, including the information that the rare artifacts you are about to see are on loan from Italy's Museo della Tortura. It says, in part:

Instruments of Torture is an exhibition featuring implements cruelly engineered to inflict unbelievable pain and suffering. But these artifacts also have a deeper significance in helping us understand who we are as human beings. By exploring why torture occurs, even in today's world, this exhibition compels us to ask:

"Are people the real instruments of torture?"

Another panel includes, in part, the following text,

In a post 9/11 world torture has become a divisive topic. . . . This exhibition . . . examines how, in specific situations, even those who deny they would ever torture another person, do exactly the opposite. . . . The exhibit encourages visitors to contemplate their own human frailty, the conditions that lead to torture, and how they can be 'up standers'—people who stand up for others—in a world that has too many by-standers. . . ."

Two large rooms are filled with contraptions and gizmos of all sizes. If you squint you can almost convince yourself that it's simply a sculpture exhibit featuring large pieces created in wood and iron and spiky bits of steel. To look closely, however, is to see and imagine dreadful stories, to behold instruments ingeniously designed to wreak havoc on human bodies. Wires and cranks and wheels and whips and hammers and chisels and spikes and . . . you name it. We've come up with it. Squeezing, flaying, poking, piercing, crushing, burning, suffocating. I want to frame it all as a distant medieval nightmare but, of course, you can read here the details about, for example, waterboarding. A crude and old-fashioned form of torture finessed into sophisticated "en-hanced interrogation" techniques by some of *our* best medical professionals, professionals from the American Psychological Association collaborating directly, according to recent reports, with the CIA and the Department of Defense. Protocols aimed at breaking down ones sense of identity, personhood.

Written on one wall is "The Ticking Time Bomb Justification." It lays out the idea that a deadly bomb is soon to explode and information *must* be extracted from the enemy. No matter the cost. It is like that TV show, *24*. It says, "We find the argument compelling—the suffering of one who might be guilty, for the benefit of many innocent people who might otherwise die. The ticking bomb scenario triggers an emotional reaction and an ethical question: Is torture justified?"

As I walk around the room I notice that *so* much here has to do with the genitals. Many devices are designed to crush the penis or lock the vagina (many deaths by infection) or pull off your limbs or your cock, to clamp off your testicles or breasts or peel off your skin in such a way that you remain alive for much of it. And our species, it appears, has been particularly creative regarding the anus. Like a bully's bull's-eye, the ass seems to invite cruelty. Countless things shoved or poked or poured piping hot into the rectum. Dear God. And, oh, over here there are lots of machines created to crush the head. Slowly. I mean, what were these people thinking?

And I have to admit that, besides my abject horror and terror, there exists within me this hitherto mentioned titillation. It jumps up inside me before I can judge or stop it. Like some primordial DNA. This frightens me about myself. The way my body will react. Become confusingly stirred as I read or see a picture or a description of cruelty. It crosses my mind how sexual in nature our manifestations of torture can be. I recall that when the photos from Abu Ghraib were released, I was repulsed and fascinated at once by those deeply disturbing images of the female soldier holding a leash, lording it over a pile of naked male prisoners. Nakedness and power and horror all intertwined. I have to wonder what in the world is going on in my own being, my own body, my own planet, as I experience at once a command to look away along with an imperative to witness. A stirring shock at this mirror of . . . us.

I WAS READING A BOOK called *The Tell-Tale Brain*, by V. S. Ramachandran. He's a neuroscientist at the University of California, San Diego, where he teaches at the Center for Brain and Cognition.

Ramachandran describes that within the prefrontal cortex regions of our brain is a class of nerve cells called *mirror neurons*. They essentially enable you to empathize with another person, allow you to take on, literally and figuratively, the point of view of another. A stranger's pain becomes your pain.

He goes on to write,

> Indian and Buddhist mystics say that there is no essential difference between self and other, and that true enlightenment comes from the compassion that dissolves this barrier. I used to think that this was just well intentioned mumbo-jumbo, but here is a neuron that doesn't know the difference between self and other. Are our brains uniquely hardwired for empathy and compassion?

I loved the sound of that. It made me ask myself, as I often do, if enlightenment is what I am really after in this life. If it's where we *sapiens* have been headed all along.

What did the angry Buddhist say to the Christian who'd just slapped him in the face?
I don't know, what did he say?
I am not turning my other cheek. I am simply, before I smack you, trying to look at your face and to remember to see it as mine.

THE ARTISTIC DIRECTOR OF THE SHAKESPEARE FESTIVAL invited me to fly out to be the guest speaker at what they called the Front Porch Series. The town was Winona, Minnesota, a quaint patch of earth on the banks of the Mississippi River. My assignment was to present a fifty-minute talk about my play and book, about the differences perhaps between crafting a story for the page and for the stage. "Talk about anything you want, really," Paul, the director, had said in his e-mail. "Folks will ask questions. It'll be fun. The fee is decent and summer in Minnesota is lovely."

I settled into a small hotel room that looked out on the mighty, muddy river. With his usual graciousness, Paul called to check in to see that I'd arrived in one piece and if I needed anything.

"All good here," I told him. "The drive from Minneapolis was dazzling; I kept weaving in and out of Wisconsin."

"Welcome to the heartland."

"Thanks. Sweet here."

Then he said,

"I hate to throw this at you, but there's a local law enforcement guy in charge of a training institute of some sort. It's part of the, ah, let me get this right, the 'National Association to Prevent Sexual Abuse of Children.' He's anxious to meet you."

"Me?" I said, looking out the window at the bright sky, noting the kerplunk in the gut at the cluster of those particular terms: children, abuse, sexual. That such a subject would have *anything at all* to do with me.

"He wants to give you a tour of the facility."

"Really? When?"

"Now."

"Oh?"

The lake up the road, the one the man at the front desk had just told me about, was shimmering in my mind. It's all I'd envisioned for the immediate future—a swim, a towel, a book. Paul read my silence.

"We'll make it short. Promise. It would be helpful for the theater, community relations and so on. They bought a block of tickets for your talk. Think you can swing it?"

"I'd rather go swimming," I said and laughed.

"Me, too," Paul responded with his own jolly chortle. "We'll make it quick."

I put my swim trunks on under my khaki pants and went to meet Paul in the lobby.

As we entered the shiny complex, which was part of the local university, the man and his family were lined up waiting for us.

"I'm Victor," he said, grabbing my hand. "This is my wife and son and daughter." The family was dressed formally, as if they'd just come from church. Victor, a dark-haired man, wore a dark suit and red tie, as did his lanky and shy-seeming son. His wife stood courteous, smiling, in a purplish dress, and his daughter was in a flowery skirt of pinks and yellows. With one hand, the girl was clasping her opposite wrist, arms a barrier across her midsection. Her stance pigeon-toed, one knee bent. Both children blushed as we shook hands. The son's face was handsome and packed with pimples; his feet shuffled in very large and shiny shoes. I imagined that, rather than standing here on a summer's day, they wished to jump in a lake as much as I. There was a solemnity as we carried out our salutations, as if they perceived me as a visiting dignitary. I felt touched and flattered and oh so awkward.

Victor gestured toward a hallway and we began to walk as he talked a mile a minute. It became clear that he was a man of great passion. That perhaps, if he spoke fast and furiously enough, he could put an end to the abuse of kids on every corner of our troubled Earth. Bless him. The speed of his speech, the fervor of his compact body were unsettling, breathtaking.

There were offices and desks, as one might expect in a training center. But then, with a sweep of Victor's arm, we entered upon the crown jewel: a mock house, a huge space built for the purpose of staging and studying scenarios of abuse. It was a sort of theater where life could be observed from beyond glass walls or some sort of two-way mirror. A playhouse, an intricate stage set with various rooms under glass. Living rooms and bedrooms and bathrooms and stairways fixed with hidden cameras, secret compartments where agents, or student agents, could observe reenactments of life and crimes unfolding. He explained that this was a central part of the National Child Protection Training Center. A place for learning the realities of what goes on, how to detect possible molestation, how to prosecute it and, most important, how to prevent these terrible violations. I didn't understand who did the acting out of scenes or if someone actually wrote scripts and situations, improvisations based on, say, the babysitter, or the visiting uncle, a father, a villain. I didn't understand really how it all worked (and didn't have it in me to ask). I walked around and peered through large windows into a fake and somehow depressing suburban home. It was as if we'd entered some Escheresque hallucination or a Pirandellian drama of our own. I had no doubt that someone smart had thought all this up, that it was born of a desire to be of service, to somehow right and prevent terrible wrongs. But I couldn't wait to get outside.

Meanwhile, Victor continued speaking at an inhuman clip, with the fervor of a radical prosecutor, like Javert in *Les Misérables*, tirelessly pursuing his enemy. "Our goal is to stamp out abuse of children. This is our mandate, our mission." He spoke as a man possessed. I wondered what *his* story might be. What fueled him? Anger? Sorrow. Love? I wondered but didn't ask.

He was talking now about the sensitivity with which children should be questioned in a courtroom, the way language should be handled in such delicate matters. "You don't use big words," he said. "You don't say 'erection' or 'flaccid.' You say, 'Was Daddy's peepee soft or hard?' 'Did he hurt you?' 'Where?'"

I glanced at the family, stoically observing. Were they as uncomfortable as I, did they feel held hostage to this overwhelming passion? Were they as astounded as I at his frankness? His work must not be new to them. They'd likely heard it all before. He began explicating the vital importance of children's rights in the courtroom. That kids compelled to testify must have safeguards, that comforts like a pet or a favorite stuffed animal must be allowed in court. That defense lawyers must adhere to guidelines, they must be taught to interrogate gently, not to intimidate. "God knows, these kids have already been through enough," he said. He spoke of fighting for legislation regarding all of this. His fervor was vivid and admirable.

I glanced at Paul, hoping we were nearing the end of our tour, when Victor turned to me.

"I'm familiar with your work," he said. "Looking forward to your presentation."

"Thanks. I'm honored you're coming."

It occurred to me in the silence that followed that he was seeking some sort of response about what we'd just seen and heard.

"This facility, this work here is incredibly impressive," I said. "Unique."

Then he asked, "Martin, what do you think about the law as it stands in regard to perpetrators? You speak from experience. You're a victim."

I stammered a moment, thinking, *I'm no victim, Victor. I'm no loser.* "I'm really . . . I'm not up on the law, I have to admit."

"But what would you do to stop these criminals? Should the laws be changed, made stricter?"

"I know the laws differ quite a bit from state to state . . ."

"What happened to your perpetrator? If you don't mind my asking."

"He was convicted at some point, back in the seventies. Not by me, though. By another boy and his family."

"Did he do much time?"

"Not really. I ultimately found out he served only a matter of months. Had to leave the state, though, I think? Not sure, but he is a registrant."

"He's become someone else's problem. They don't change you know. Statistics show. They suffer from this affliction. But how do we stop them?"

I shrugged. His family looked on. How often, I wondered again, had they stood in silence and listened to this?

"Well, arrest, of course," I said. "And, I understand there are more programs now, more sophisticated ways to help perpetrators. I haven't thought about the legal aspects. I'm not very political that way. Of course, protecting children is a priority, but in terms of how the law works I'm afraid I have no clear answers. I guess as a writer I deal more in ambiguity." I fumbled through a few more half thoughts, saying something about complexity, about the greater awareness I should no doubt have.

"You must have some sense of what is a just and effective punishment?"

"I don't, actually," I said. "People are sick and . . . every situation is different and . . . I don't know."

"The bottom line is, they need to be incapacitated," Victor said. "That's my opinion."

"You mean stiffer sentences?"

"I mean castration," he said.

I saw that he was absolutely serious. He expounded, perhaps because my face betrayed some shock, some confusion at the sound of the word.

"In my opinion," he said, "castration is the best way. It protects children and society and, well, ultimately, it's merciful for offenders because it takes away their desire at the root, eradicates the obsession. It's actually the humane thing to do."

I glanced at Paul, wondering what he was making of this. I couldn't tell. Victor's family remained quiet.

I was aware that I was awestruck. This whole thing, the place, his fury, felt somehow Greek to me. I mean the kind of huge emotion that one associates with classic dramatic characters—the ones who don't fool around when they get really pissed. You know, the wife who makes mincemeat out of the kids as payback for her husband's infidelity. I mean, the Greeks, they know from rage.

"Thank you again," Paul said as we all shook hands and went on our way. The attractive young son blushed again as I squeezed his hand. My face flushed, too, and my chest rumbled with feelings too many and complicated to discern. What was it like for this young man, I wondered, and for his young silent sister, to live with a father so fierce, so dead set on protecting the young from harm?

I STUFF THE REQUISITE PROPS INTO MY BACKPACK: a dog-eared journal, a framed photo of me at twelve, a CD of James Taylor tunes, a bottle of water. Assuming there's a stool at the venue to perch upon, a light or two to point at my face and a halfway-willing audience, I'm good to go. I know the play by heart, can recite the eighty minutes of it at the drop of a hat. Gypsy storyteller. It's a tale I lived, dug up, wrote down, and have now rehearsed and performed and rehearsed again . . . to death.

I hoist my pack and head out of the apartment to the corner of our street where one can usually nab a gypsy cab—the only taxis hailable in our lower-rent, way-uptown neighborhood.

Within a few moments I'm sitting in a large Chevy that smells faintly of gasoline, moving west across the George Washington Bridge.

"Where are you from?" I ask through the Plexiglas.

"Santo Domingo," the driver replies.

"Beautiful there, I hear."

"*Si, si, precioso.* You should visit."

"Lots of sun and beach, right?"

"*Si. Si.* Fine weather. And you?"

"Colorado."

"Beautiful state I hear?"

"Yes. So why are we here?"

He grins. "Work," he says, his dark eyes catching mine in the rearview mirror. "*Dinero.*"

"I hear that," I tell him.

We arrive at the center of a small campus composed of low-lying brick buildings. On one side of the handsome quad a row of Japanese cherry blossoms are in full bloom, bow upon bow draped with flowers—bright pink against the blue of day. Less than an hour from Manhattan, it is astonishingly quiet. Could be Iowa. A shame, I think, to go into a windowless theater.

The driver steps out of the car as I do and says, as if reading my mind,

"*Tranquilo.*"

"*Si.*" I hand him cash. "May I have a receipt?"

He reaches into the car and rips one from a pad.

"You can fill it in, OK? *Buenos dias.*"

"*Gracias.*"

He pulls away.

A statue of the Virgin Mary is plopped in the middle of things, snow white opposite the blushing blossoms. Though I don't know the history of this institution, I'm figuring Catholics—always an eye for real estate, for the shaping of young souls—are at the root of this place. Students with satchels move briskly along the crisscross of sidewalks, into and out of various doors. I stand and watch. Fighting an urge to sit beneath the trees, I move toward the auditorium. I'm due within. Signed a contract. Need the *dinero*.

I've been booked, along with a speaker who will follow my performance, as part of a seminar for mental health professionals of northern New Jersey. This is the kind of gathering where, so I am told, they will receive continuing-education credit for attending. Like many of the groups I've performed for, there is an acronym for this crowd but I've forgotten it now. Some do stick with me: SNAP (Survivors Network of Those Abused by Priests). AA-SECT (American Association of Sexuality Educators, Counselors, and Therapists)—the most liberal gang I've performed for.

Their conference in sunny Phoenix was titled "Some Like It Hot." And recently there was the MS (Male Survivor) conference at John Jay College of Criminal Justice. I recall stepping out to get a cup of tea before my show began. I passed three students who'd just come in from a light rain. They appeared to be on their way to class, noses buried in smartphones. A young woman in a red windbreaker raised her device toward the "Male Survivor" sign in the lobby.

"What's that?" she asked. "What are *they* surviving?"
A boy in a fedora looked over at the conference poster.
"Who knows?"
A second girl, blond strands damp against her forehead, said, "Yeah. Everyone's got their shit."

I find the stage and the stool and the stage manager, who dims the house and ignites the stage lights. The audience goes quiet and I begin. A smooth performance, it seems, but for the disturbance of latecomers sneaking into the auditorium. Eighty minutes down and I stop talking; I take a bow and then a seat in the front row.

The speaker steps up. Her name is Patricia Sherman. A therapist. Early forties, I'd say. I like her immediately. She's beautiful and laughs easily, recounting a silly scene of serving lumpy oatmeal to her grumpy youngest that morning as she weaves through an explanation of her work with trauma victims. Her blouse is cream colored, her skirt maroon. She wears gold earrings and bejeweled bifocals. She strikes me as combination librarian and lawyer. She has terrific posture (something my mother always pointed out as a profoundly laudable trait). She's come now to the part where she tells of being raped repeatedly by her father from the time she was three. She leans into the microphone, her voice rising and falling on flutters of breath as if whispering a bedtime story to a group of restless kids. Big kids with BlackBerrys, checking messages, slipping in and out of the side doors of the theater. She tells how her mother turned a blind eye, a numb heart. How she was forced to terminate pregnancies as a mere girl and how all of this led to disaster in her adult life and relationships. Until she found the right help, that is, and uncovered the strength and insight and love to cope with what happened. She's now long married, a mother of two. She covers all this ground with breathtaking economy and matter-of-fact dignity. I wonder how much time she's spent assembling the self she presents this fine May morning. She wraps up by saying,

"We must guard against our own pessimism and harbor true hope that our clients can heal from even the worst kinds of violence. There exists an army of us *survivors*. But I have come to prefer another term. It has been suggested that those who have experienced abuse and survived be called *transcenders*."

There's polite applause. The stage manager sets two folding chairs on the stage. Patricia gestures for me to step up and take a seat next to her.

Hands go up. A young woman addresses me.

Isn't it painful, sir, to tell your story again and again, to relive the past like that?

"Well," I say, "what I've created is a piece of theater, a living event. The material is from my life and true—as best I can render truth in language and gesture, but I'm not reliving the past so much as conjuring questions with you in the present. Human questions about reconciliation, about letting go, about how we might gain some authority over what has happened in our lives. There is a lot of joy in communing like this through storytelling."

Are you still a Catholic?

"I rarely go into church, but I'd have to say the church is in me. It feels nearly . . . racial. Complicated. I feel affection for my upbringing even as I feel disgust with the whole Catholic mess. The thing is, I swallowed so much of the milk of Mother Church—sin, redemption, the whole nine yards—it's in the marrow and seems to spill out in my writing."

An older lady stands, removes her glasses.

Is telling the story, the writing of it, cathartic?

"Insofar as writing and creating work is a release, yes, there is that. Aristotle talked of catharsis in drama as the evocation of pity and fear in order to bring about harmony between men and gods. My hope, I think, is that there's an element *for you* of finding harmony, a moment of epiphany from the work. I hate to think of this enterprise as, you know, *self-help*. But what's interesting is that catharsis, its root, is as a medical term. From the Greek *katharein*, meaning 'to cleanse. Purify.' It was an herb, a laxative. . . ."

There are a few titters, just as I'd hoped. I've used the line before. I've been honing and rehearsing these answers at my countless post-show Q-and-A's along the way.

". . . yes, really, a medical term for purging of the bowels or for the menstrual cycle. You know . . . a process that asks to be repeated, so to speak! It seems to say that our work here is an ongoing practice that keeps on wanting, needing, to happen. Things build up, get plugged up, and need purging. The ritual of theater, for instance, storytelling, is one kind of purging. Purification? A daily seeking of harmony or simply trying to find a way to be present to . . . to *what is*."

What do you mean by forgiveness?

"Different things at different junctures, I guess. Lately, I've been thinking how it's not a onetime thing, you know? *Forgive* and it's all over and done. Maybe it's more like a door you choose to walk though saying, OK, I'm going to try to move this way. I'm going to give this to myself, this release from the past. This compassion for my self, for the kid I was, the man I am, and for Bob, for being the utterly screwed-up being he was at that time."

I talk and talk and I feel the vibration from within to out, the sound of my voice center stage traveling into the room and I think, "Yes, they are *humming* with me and I with them and this is good and we are *one*." This is my mission. I'm exactly where I'm meant to be. How funny it happens to be with shrinks in New Jersey, but so it is, and I take in the rapt faces, the cocked heads, the words falling like marbles from my mouth, rolling toward wisdom, toward truth. Oh! I feel an expansive sense of being centered, of being a heroic fellow traveler, a Buddha doing good work, dropping a few pearls and a man's hand shoots up, his eyes pinched in a way that tell me he's not buying. He looks to me like Freud or a Freud impersonator. Gray beard, oval-lensed glasses, tweed suit. Male authority.

"Young man," he begins, "the way you describe the scene of confronting your perpetrator, and finding compassion there . . ."

"Yes?"

"Well, surely anger was a part of that meeting. Were you able to express your outrage?"

A sudden rush of blood surges from bowels to gullet. "Of course I've been angry," I say, but my throat clogs. I go silent. No words but the hate, sudden fucking absolute *hate*, that I am inside this dark hall on a spring day. The sudden surety that my life should be other than it is, anywhere but the place, the moment I am in. A lost boy in front of bearded man as the easy light of cherry blossoms blooms just beyond the brick, as I stand in the muck of a story born thirty years ago getting paid six hundred measly dollars to *perform* for, to convince a bunch of restless therapists how salient my redemptive woe might be for their extra credit. Enough, Marty! No more spinning elegant sentences out of this shit. What are you doing? You loser!

You're not wanted on a movie set, not the rich and famous Martin you dreamed you'd be. "Whatever happened to Moran, he had such promise? Oh, he's out peddling his sad old show. He could have been something, but he just didn't have it. Not a big enough gun." The poisonous refrain. The *might-have-beens*, the *if-onlys* engulf the air, swamp the soul, and I know beyond doubt that I am broken and I am staring at Freud, at his salt-and-pepper beard, as I tumble down tunnels, as I move my eyes to the back wall, the sun blazing there just beyond the dim auditorium. I'm a failure and every scrap of my life, of my energy, is constructed to keep at bay the mean fear that this is the fact of the matter. That success was derailed all those years ago, the moment I wanted, allowed this most private place in me to be fondled. Can't let the kid off the hook, can you? I was weak then and am now and I pray, literally fucking pray, for the stage to open and swallow the strutting actor. Please. Oh God, when, how do we get free of—

"Wouldn't you say, young man," his voice breaks through to where I am sinking, "wouldn't you say that there isn't a day in your life that you don't, in some way, think about this man, 'Bob,' who violated you?"

"Let's move on," comes the voice of my copresenter. "Next question?"

MY FATHER POINTED TO AN EMPTY VEHICLE at the side of the road. "Could bake a twenty-pound turkey in there," he said. "Must be at least 110 degrees."

We were stuck at a red light in a long line of cars spewing fumes. The world-famous Las Vegas Strip undulated in the distance, sun drenched and hazy through the fierce midday heat.

We sat.

Idle.

I fiddled with the radio.

"Christ, this traffic!" he said, for the third or maybe fourth time since we began our slow journey across the hurried city. "These signals are interminable. Would it hurt for them to synchronize the damn things? Jesus. Who *are* all these people?"

"Lots of Mormons have been moving in. I read that somewhere," I said. "And Catholics. Lots of religions coming to town."

"Gambling is still chief among them, believe you me," he said. "Wasn't so crowded as this when we moved here ten years ago."

He dug into his breast pocket for a cigarette.

"Dad, this is a nonsmoking car."

"How the hell will Hertz know? They have cameras? Communists."

The rasp in his throat was the old song of the western-style, die-hard Republican he was. His stubbornness irritated and charmed me in equal measure. There my dad sat, his handsome face a drape of wrinkles, his teeth gone missing, one of his eyes bloodshot and swollen nearly shut. But still, the glint, the grit.

"Dad? Please. The rent-a-car company has asked . . . it gives me a headache, actually. Can you just wait till we get there?"

"I can't be smoking *right* before my oil change," he said, referring to his thrice-weekly trip to the clinic, his date with dialysis. He gave me a wink and the wry glint of him sailed across the car. Amazing how it still showed up, this undying Irish charisma flashing through a body gone so heavy with defeat. "They'll give me hell if they see it. Or smell it."

"Dad, they're gonna smell it."

"Just a few puffs, Tiger. I'll blow it right out the window."

He cracked it open. I cranked the AC.

"Yeah, it's not just retirees like us," he declared, "sick of shoveling snow. Lots of young people are moving in. And so lots of kids, lots of new schools being built, along with everything else. Look."

He pointed past me over to a shiny white building across the oncoming traffic.

"Wow. Beautiful structure," I said. "Looks new."

"It is. Brand-spanking state-of-the-art library."

"That's cool."

"Only one problem. Guess what it's missing."

"Customers?" I deduced, glancing at the empty parking lot.

"Books." He chortled, exhaled. We stopped at another light.

Smoke filled the car. I didn't actually hate it. The scent had been an element of his presence since I was a kid; a kind of home base. Standing outside after church, or at the foot of a mountain waiting to get on the ski lift, or on the back patio after mowing the lawn—the whiff of fresh grass and Philip Morris defined a Saturday afternoon. His ways were ever quiet back then, his fire hidden, and so smoke a knowable aspect of the man.

Though I saw that now, rather than Philip Morris, he was lighting up a brandless cigarette. The kind he and his wife,

Barbara, purchased in bargain quantity from the roadside market run by a local Indian tribe. They were on a fixed income, after all, watching their pennies. They've worked hard and they own a home, but I could sense their worry over every dollar spent. I felt for them and felt how heavy my heart had become: the weight of this parental visit, of this ghastly metropolis, which appeared before me as a heap of compulsive behavior rising up from the desert. It simply didn't compute that this was where he chose to live. I knew he missed Denver—missed his old friends, the large oak trees, the familiar streets and family. He seemed unmoored here. That was *my* judgment and whenever I brought up the possibility of his moving back to our hometown, he shook his head and said how the Denver he knew no longer existed. "Not my city," he said. "What I knew of home is gone. Gone."

The signal finally went green and we moved eastward toward the clinic. I wished to be chipper, to keep up some sort of conversation.

"Want to get lunch after dialysis?"

"Maybe. May just want to nap. The two highlights of my day, you know? My hot shower and my afternoon nap."

He tossed his cigarette, rolled up the window, and said,

"See that Casino over there?"

"Which?"

"The old one. Up ahead on the right."

"With the sign busted?"

"Yeah."

"Sad-looking place," I said.

"Local joint. You know, you know that small inheritance I talked to you kids about?"

I nodded, vaguely recalling a vague mention.

"Well," he continued with a little cough, "well . . ." I suddenly realized this was hard for him; whatever it was he is trying to say.

"Stupidest thing."

"What do you mean?"

"Well, they got most of it."

"What? Who?"

"They got it. Nickel at a time. Down the drain. It's gone."

"You mean your savings?

He nodded.

"Dad, I don't think any of us were really thinking about . . . I mean, don't worry but . . . ?" I began.

He was quiet.

"Are you OK? Do you have what you . . . Are you in trouble?"

He stared ahead. Said nothing.

"Dad?"

"It's been hard," he said. "She disappears for hours. The credit card bills show up. I tell her we can't pay and that she will have to go to jail. I mean, I try to scare her, that it's serious. She cries. We pay. I don't know what else to do. It's gone."

We drove along. He seemed helpless. I didn't know what to say or do. It was one of those moments: Was I meant to step in as ally, as adult? Not simply play the child? I realized that he was reaching out. More than the shock of it, I realized that I was touched he was trusting me with this.

"Dad, what can I do?"

"Nothing. We'll get through."

"Are you sure?"

"Damn chip," he said.

"Chip?"

"That's all it is. You know, it's all one giant machine—a massive corporate computer. Makes me so *angry*. When you stick your quarters or dimes in there, you're playing a rigged machine. The whole town, the whole world, is run by a computer chip and you can't win. You can't. I just realized it one day. It hit me. That this *thing* was playing me; like their device had become a part of my own brain. Implanted by *them*. And I *allowed* it! I had given them control and I felt . . . suddenly, you know, duped. Pissed off. The whole thing is so foolish when you look at it. Maybe there are a few talented card players out there that can really beat the system, but mainly we are bunch of sheep being led to the slaughter by these greedy jerks. It's like they reduce you to a pinpoint of desire. Sucking your blood, sucking the money right out of your wallet. And I felt so disgusted and that was it."

"You quit?"

"Yeah. I quit," he said, his voice sharp, clarified by ire. "Don't want to be a damn cog. Couldn't stand the thought of it."

His eyes, his words were keen, his intelligence beaming through. It was good, I realized, to hear him talk like this. I felt linked to him in such a human way, the way of shared plight. I blurted out,

"I admire that you, that you stopped, Dad. I don't really get the gambling thing, never did, but I can tell you, Dad, I've got my own things, you know. My . . . compulsions. I mean, I relate. You know, the desire to escape."

I was thinking of, but not saying out loud, my years of pot smoking. Of my crazed trances trolling the Internet, looking for ever-more-beautiful naked bodies. Talk about a chip in your brain, about becoming a digital cog fused with the pixelated images spinning out from a giant wheel of desire, a craving to be snatched at any cost from the present. Compulsions, I surmise, born of my boyhood sex. I don't get gambling, but I can picture the liftoff, the orgasm, when the bells ring and you feel you are recognized for one high and oblivious moment as the chosen one, the *winner!* The explosion of pleasure, of a wild transcendence. I know about searching mindlessly for that jackpot, for that hope that my mind will blow off and away. And then the letdown, leaving me as exhausted and bankrupt as Dad was talking of now. I know from addiction.

"I relate, Dad. I don't want to be . . . to be a cog, either."

"Yeah, well. It's just stupid."

"Dad? How can I help?'

"Nothing you can do, really."

"But she . . . ?'

"She has a problem."

I left a space if he wanted to say more.

Silence.

I won't hear her side of the story. She and I were not good at talking, but I knew she was doing a lot of heavy lifting taking care of Dad with his deteriorating condition. She was doing her best. She had health insurance from her many years of hard work. He depended on that. She was a good person. She loved him. It had to be tough for her.

"Dad? Do you have enough money? Are you OK?"

More silence. His face was clouded.

"It's bad," he said. "But you know . . ." He trailed off. "This is marriage. Twenty some years of it. I love her."

"Do you talk?" He shrugged.

"Do you want me to talk to her?" I asked.

He was silent. And I thought, yes, he does. He's alone in this, and he needs an ally. He began to cough, uncontrollably. He reached for another cigarette.

"Dad? Could you maybe not . . . ?

"Just a couple of puffs, Tiger. Before we get there."

Just one more before he'd have to fold himself into a chair for his three-hour oil change.

The clinic did, in fact, look like a garage. One story, concrete, large sliding doors. Just the place to roll in and have your engine checked.

The attending nurse, a tall black man with a clipboard, asked Dad if he'd been eating well.

"Oatmeal," Dad replied. "Lots of oatmeal."

"Is that all you eat, Mr. Moran?"

"Just about."

"You exercising?"

"A vigorous shower in the morning."

"Been smoking?"

"Who? Me?"

Dad shrugged and offered his toothless leprechaun grin. The nurse couldn't resist a quick smile amid his act of exasperation. He gave Dad a little whack on the shoulder with his clipboard. Dad raised his hands in mock defense. It seemed this was their routine, their little *lazzi*. The nurse played stern now, wagging a finger. "Come on now, Mr. Moran. Take this seriously."

"This is my son," Dad gestured toward me. "He's a Broadway actor."

"Really?"

"Sometimes," I said. "Not lately."

"Can he sit here for a few?" Dad asked. The nurse nodded toward a stool next to Dad's appointed lounge chair. "Not for long, though. It's against the rules."

I sat as Dad got strapped in. Another male nurse took his blood pressure and vitals and then tubes were hooked up. The fluids began to move out and in.

There were TV sets and Barcalounger beds running along two walls. Fifteen, maybe twenty folks were receiving fresh blood as they slept, read, or watched TV.

"You want a magazine? Or the TV on?"

Dad shook his head, already drowsy. Soon he was dozing.

I went to the waiting room, where some other folks, chauffeurs, relatives, hired help, sat reading *People* and *Time*. The vague smell of medical sadness hung in the air, the business of staying alive a little longer.

I got restless after an hour or so and went back in to sit near Dad. No one seemed to mind. He was awake, just staring at the ceiling. Then he noticed me, smiled a bit.

"Done soon," he said.

I sat and took his hand.

Suddenly there was a commotion. A large double door at the back, on the far end of the room, flew open. It gave way to a rear parking lot. An ambulance was there. Quiet but lights flashing. A three-man EMT crew walked in. They moved slowly so it didn't seem to be an emergency, but they made a beeline to one of the beds on the far end of the room where a curtain had been drawn. They went behind it. There was a quiet bustle there for a time. Long enough that Dad and I turned away and our thoughts and talk moved to other things. Lunch. A stop at the store. But soon the crew came out rolling a gurney, a body on it, covered. Anonymous in its facelessness, they steered it toward the parking lot.

"He gets to leave by the special door today," Dad whispered, his face placid. "Off into the desert." I watched his eyes follow the body and then he turned to me. There was his twinkle and, then, a shrug. "Happens here all the time."

SIBA AND I ARE SEATED ON A WOODEN BENCH where Wall Street meets the East River. There's a large dock to our right where a fleet of fat boats, bright yellow trimmed with black, busily glide in and back out, like large and lumbering bumblebees.

"Ferry boats?" Siba asks.

"Yes, water taxis."

It's fall, a crisp October afternoon, 2008. We'd arranged to meet near the sandwich shop where he's found a job washing dishes and making occasional deliveries. He has only a small window of time in his busy schedule. Monday through Saturday he works at the sandwich shop 7 a.m. to 4 p.m., and then, most days, he heads back to the community college in Jersey City for English classes from 7 to 9. In between, he studies.

The sun blazes at our backs. It's perfectly poised above the cluster of downtown skyscrapers so that, just now, its light is setting the surface of the river afire. From where we sit it seems that, rather than floating on water, the boats are gliding through gold.

"*C'est genial ici,*" says Siba.

"Brilliant," I agree, nudging him toward English. I point to my mouth. "Brilliant."

"Brilliant," he repeats with his guttural roll of an r and l's that come out like y's. "I work two blocks away," he gestures behind us toward the west, "and I never even knew this river was here!" He laughs.

"Your English . . . ," I say.

"Improving?" he asks. In English.

It's eight months now that I've known him. We don't meet often but he's recently acquired a cell and when it works, when he's able to pay for the minutes, we check in by phone. Every conversation begins the exact same way. He asks,

How is your Mother?

Fine.

And your brother?

Good.

His health is OK?

Better, thanks.

Good. And your sisters?

He remembers, it seems, anything I happen to share about my family. My brother David's struggles with diabetes and the blues, my sisters' kids. I want to ask him about his family, of course, but I dare not. If he had news I suppose he'd tell me. I always ask about his asylum case. There are many steps to the process, many months of waiting. But he's filled out every form and shown up for every interview. He's been diligent. And, thankfully, he has a good lawyer.

I know from his I-589 that Siba's birthday is a few days away and I pull a small gift from my pack.

"*Bon anniversaire.*"

"*Monsieur Martin! Non.*"

He unwraps it. Two books. A large-print, young-adult version of the story of the *Titanic* and a short biography of Barack Obama.

"*Titanic!*" he exclaims.

"You know the story?"

"Yes. From school."

He pulls his glasses from his pocket, takes them from their case, and cleans them, carefully, before putting them on and opening the book about the doomed ship.

"*Bonjour*, Professor Siba," I say, which makes him laugh.

The glasses look great on him. We'd bought them together a few months before. The purchase happened on a whim, really, a chance accident. I'd gone to meet him for lunch in Jersey City one afternoon not far from the house that he shares with five, sometimes six other African refugees. We walked slowly from the PATH station in Journal Square to a café run by a Pakistani man. Siba was limping slightly. He'd twisted his ankle in a weekend soccer game, nothing serious, he assured me.

When we reached the restaurant, I pulled from my pack an article I'd clipped from the *Times*. It was titled "At The Sudan-Chad Border." It included photos of soldiers lounging in the desert landscape and a lengthy piece about the current state of affairs in Siba's part of the world. I thought he might find the news and pictures of interest. That he might be impressed to see how we Americans are keeping up with events in his faraway homeland. The moment I set it on the table, he began to study it keenly.

Our chicken and rice with lentil sauce arrived. The Pakistani man kept looking over from the front counter, asking,

"How is it? You like it?"

We nodded.

Siba kept squinting, pointing at things in the article he seemed to recognize.

"You sure the sauce OK?" The man inquired again. "I have others."

"OK," we assured him.

"Just let us know." He nodded toward the waitress, who grinned. I asked where she was from. "Turkey," she told us. "How long have you been here?" I asked. "Almost two years."

New York City is known, of course, for its wide mix of cultures, but walking the streets in parts of New Jersey can be like a visit to the UN. You see saris and headdresses and turbans and robes and all sorts of colorful glimpses of global culture. When I began volunteering at the International Institute of New Jersey in late 2007, I remember my friend Sara telling me some of the statistics. How this corner of the United States serves as a gateway for thousands of immigrants, as it has for centuries. Ellis Island is only a couple of miles away, as are JFK and Newark airports. When I am out late and take a taxi home, invariably I catch a glimpse of our world reflected through the driver's rearview mirror, through the mostly dark eyes of a talkative soul telling me of Jericho, Tashkent, Lima, Lahore, Bangladesh, Ethiopia.

As Siba and I ate our lunch I began to read and translate the article as best I could with the help of the small French-English dictionary I'd brought along. It reported how the already unstable region was thrown into further turmoil with the recent upheaval in Darfur, and how Chadian rebel factions were receiving arms from Sudan. Rocket launchers, antitank and antiaircraft missiles. When I read out certain names—Idriss Deby, Mahamat Nouri, a Chadian rebel leader—Siba's eyes brightened.

"Yes, yes," he said. "Deby is the president. He is Zakhawan. They do not like us. We are Goran. There has been a long, terrible struggle between our groups."

He squinted at the print, rubbing his head, his eyes and temple. I thought he might be upset, recalling the circumstances of his region, his arrest.

"Are you OK?" I asked.

"*Oui. Oui.*"

"You have a headache?"

He nodded and said, "My head hurts. It hurts when I read."

"Close your eyes. I'll keep reading," I suggested.

After a bit he looked again at the paper, squinting, and it was then, on a whim, that I handed him my reading glasses. He put them on and let out a funny cry.

"*C'est claire!*" he said. His face brightened. He pointed to the newsprint. "*C'est claire.*" It's clear!

"Siba, maybe . . . maybe you need glasses?" I said. He cocked his head. What an idea. "We should get you to an eye doctor. But, you know, we could get you some reading glasses right now."

He looked surprised. We paid our check, thanked the café owner, and walked the few blocks back toward Journal Square. Along the way we passed a beloved statue of Jackie Robinson.

"You know who that is?"

"First black player in American baseball. Like Obama will be the first black president," Siba said.

We stood by the display rack at Duane Reade. Siba was finicky picking out and trying on several pairs of glasses. Once we figured out what strength we should get, he made me laugh as he kept looking up and posing toward the little mirror atop the display rack. We spent a long time discussing different frames and colors. When he picked up the gold-rimmed pair that he finally chose, he looked at himself for a long time. His expression grave. Finally he smiled and turned to me.

"Monsieur Martin, I like these."

"Me, too."

We got a little case along with the glasses. It wasn't expensive, maybe twenty-five bucks. I had that awkward feeling when I pulled out my AmEx card—a piece of plastic that seemed to set us worlds apart.

We walked to the station. Before I got on my train back to Manhattan, I handed him the *Times* article and the small French-English dictionary we'd been using.

"Thanks, Monsieur Martin. You wasted your whole day here."

"Don't say that. It is great spending time with you. Hey, you look like a professor in those glasses," I'd said. "Professor Siba."

"*Grand merci*, Martin." He laughed his laugh, shaking his head as we parted.

And now here he is, carefully cleaning his glasses, putting the case back in his pocket, focusing on the text and photos of the long-ago tragedy of the *Titanic*.

"Crazy story," he says.

"You know I once did a play, a musical about the *Titanic*."

"A musical?" he asks.

I nod and start to recount a bit about the Broadway version of the story but his attention is fully on the book and now on the birthday card that I had tucked inside.

"What's this?"

"Just good wishes for your birthday."

He opens it. On the cover of the card is a photo of the Front Range of the Rocky Mountains. He stares at it.

"That's where I am from." I tell him. "Way in the West. *Mon patrie, mon village natal.*"

"Mountains."

"Yes."

"But it's cold," he says, pointing at the snow-mantled peaks. He pulls his mouth into a frown.

"Yeah, it gets chilly there."

"I don't like the cold. Is it far from here?"

"About two thousand miles."

"So far?"

"Not as far as your home."

He looks out at the river.

"You are lucky to be born here, Martin. Here you have *justice*."

He says it with such reverence. Such weight. It's as if I've never actually heard the word until now. Then he asks,

"Where is the Statue of Liberty from here?"

I point behind us. "The other side of all these buildings."

"I'd like to go there one day."

"Well, we'll go," I say.

He slips the card back into the book.

"*Merci*, Martin."

"*Un grand plaisir*, professor."

We sip our drinks, watch the boats coming and going. It's nearing rush hour. He needs to get his train across the Hudson to get to school, and so we begin our walk up Wall Street. He stops and points up at a skyscraper with darkly tinted windows.

"On Saturdays," he says, "I get to deliver sandwiches here." He's grinning. "They come down to meet me, or sometimes I go in and all the way up to the offices. The people are very nice." He describes a secretary from Ohio who usually meets him on the thirtieth floor. He recounts how they shake hands and how each time they meet she teaches him a word or two of English. I picture the secretary, wonder if she has any inkling of the story of the young man who delivers lunch.

We pass Trinity, the old church tucked away near Ground Zero. We pause at the cemetery where a piece of one of the towers came down like a spear and stuck in the ground amid the old graves. I tell Siba the story and then we walk past the cranes at work in the huge, empty space and join the many moving toward the PATH. When we get to the entrance I say,

"Call me, OK?"

"I will, Martin. Tell your family hello from me."

THE SUN HAD JUST SET AND I WAS STUCK IN THE MIDDLE of Sunset Boulevard, waiting to perform what seemed an impossible feat: a left turn into the parking lot of Book Soup. The lot looked terribly remote across two lanes of merciless traffic. I could see the perfect spot to ditch my rental car and be just on time for the reading. But there was no green arrow, no break in the heat and haze, the rising fumes of a late-summer day.

It'd been six days since the memoir was officially released. I was bouncing through my first hours as a published person. Racing through a modest book tour in hopes of boosting thus-far-modest sales. I was thinking what section of the story I might read, mustering gumption to make the daredevil turn, considering a trip around the block to find a parking garage, when my cellphone rang. I shouldn't have, but I grabbed it. It was Carolyn, my younger sister, her voice wobbly.

"Marty?"

"Yeah?"

"Dad died."

"When?"

"About an hour ago."

I don't recall making the turn. I do recall parking the car, turning off the ignition, sitting there picturing Dad's pained face when I last saw him, lying in a Vegas hospital bed only days before, struggling to recover from hip surgery, the nurse assuring us he would be fine in a day or two. I got out of the car and moved toward the bookstore. "Do it for Dad," my sister had said when I told her I was just about to do an event. Amy and Suzette, two dear friends, were standing outside. "Are you all right?" Amy asked immediately. "My dad just died." They stood with me quietly for a time before we walked in. The lady in charge caught my eye, pointed to her watch, and waved me toward the podium. Folding chairs squeezed between tall shelves of wall-to-wall books. I stood and talked about the making of the memoir, the story that insisted on being told. I kept glancing at the many books, seeing my father clad in his blue button-down oxford and khakis, his young and nimble self curled on the floor, holding a book, reading. Always reading.

In the immediate hours and days that followed his death, I kept riffling through our last times together. The last time we ate together, the last time we'd skied, our last phone conversation. Which, as best I can recall, went like this:

"I'll be traveling for a little while."

"Another acting job?" he asked.

"No, going off to promote the, you know, the book I wrote. It comes out next week. I'll stop in Vegas to see you if time allows."

"I'd like that, Tiger."

I could hear his exhale, could picture the column of smoke ascending. I searched for something to fill the space, the gap where mention of the memoir now hung. He'd told me long ago that he couldn't, wouldn't ever read it. It would be *too much*, he'd said, and I didn't press him.

So now in what would turn out to be our last real conversation, I asked something about the weather, about the Broncos, when he interjected,

"I've had some calls, you know."

"Calls?

"From friends. In Denver."

"Yeah?"

"There've been articles. About your . . . your story."

"I know."

There had been several appearing along the way in the Colorado papers in relation to the exploding abuse scandal. Even about the specific Catholic summer camp, Saint Malo, where I'd first met counselor Bob.

"I guess you've caused a bit of a stir," Dad said.

"I guess."

"What a *mess*, all that," he added.

I could feel my blood, my body quicken, with the injection of *the subject*. There was a long pause and then he said,

"I hear you're a pretty good writer."

"Working on it, Dad."

"Good for you. Tight bright light right."

He often used this phrase in relation to his own work, his many years as a journalist for the *Rocky Mountain News*. His byline—identical to mine, as we share our name—never failed to give me a jolt of pride.

More silence across the wire.

Then,

"How in the world did that all happen, anyway?"

I was in my living room. I leaned forward in the chair.

"You mean—?" I began.

"Yes," he said.

I heard a reply in my head but didn't utter it. *You mean, what happened with that guy who made me gay?* A notion my older sister told me my father had suggested on the one occasion they had discussed the "mess." Instead, I asked,

"With that counselor?"

"Yeah."

"Um, well . . . it's really complicated. That's why I wrote a book, I guess." (*Why don't you just read it?* I wanted to say. Even though I understood. I knew it was all . . . *too much*.)

"But *how* did it happen?" he asked again.

What do you say to that question?

It . . .

It was an accident, Dad.

It was fate.

He . . .

He was charming

He was a fucking criminal.

He was charismatic.

He looked amazing in his Levi's 501s.

He was ill.

I . . .

I was clueless.

I was lonely.

I was young.

I had a body.

I accepted the invitation.

I wanted to go to the mountains.

I thought he really liked me.

I was weak.

I was scared.

I was a prime target.

I was your son.

And, of all the things tumbling around in my head, what dropped out of my mouth was,

"I don't know, Dad. I guess I wanted attention."

"Well, guess you got what you wanted."

And then he chuckled.

And in that moment, leaning forward in the chair in my New York apartment, I felt a wretched little wave of relief. His odd chuckle, though born of discomfort, seemed to burst an old and terrible tension, seemed to say, hey, we're just two fellas, frat brothers, bantering over past peccadillos. Pals intimate enough to talk sex. But, oh God, when I recall it now, it is with an admixture of sorrow and anger. Sorrow that I took this for closeness and fury that he (that I) could view the thing as laughable. And then, just before we hung up, he said,

"I'm happy to think, Tiger, that before I die, the name Martin Moran will be on the binding of a book."

It was released on June 15, 2005.

He died six days later.

MY BROTHER, DAVE, met me at the Las Vegas airport to drive me to Dad's funeral. He'd been living with our father for some time. Dave was thirty-eight years old then and had been at loose ends, moving among Colorado, New Mexico, and even some months in Montana, bouncing between ideas of how and where to make a living, a life. Dad and Barbara were both struggling with their health and so for several months they'd given Dave a roof while he agreed to be of help, supporting them in practical ways.

He'd written an entry about these months with Dad and Barbara in a journal of his that I later found:

The parallel life forces of my father and his wife—in the throes of decay . . . frail doesn't come to mind rather, tired. Tired of their lives, their lives shrinking and they powerless to prevent the dwindling . . .

Dave was standing just outside baggage claim, squinting in the Vegas sun. When he saw me, he tossed his cigarette, waved, and held out a dark-blue tie.

"You got my message," I said.

"Yup. Here ya go. Put this on."

"Thanks, man."

We walked silently to the car. It smelled of Dad, his cigarettes, and Irish Spring. A melancholy cocktail. Dave filled me in. How Dad, while still in the hospital recovering from hip surgery, was wheeled to dialysis one afternoon. How, in a small back room of the local hospital, all alone, his heart abruptly stopped as he was getting his oil change. An alarm went off, Dave was told. But by then it was over.

We arrived at the funeral home. Dave remained in the lobby saying hello to a few neighbors while I, thankfully, had a few quiet moments alone with Dad in a sort of makeshift chapel. Though there was an organist behind a beige curtain, playing "Danny Boy" off key. In Catholic tradition, his casket was open. I knelt at his side and placed my hand over his silent heart, upon his wool sweater. Dead and gone but the warmth and steady kindness of him was there, it seemed, woven into the fabric of his pullover. Irish-born wool it was, of which he was proud; a deep shade of green. He held an abiding affection for the old country, of which he often talked, but like many Irish Americans had never in his life managed to visit. It's a stab of sadness that he and I didn't somehow make that trip together.

I stepped out of the chapel and into the lobby and immediately spotted Barbara beyond the large, tinted plate-glass window. She was moving through the mortuary parking lot all alone, dragging a green oxygen tank on a little wagon.

Though I was never sure where we stood, I was feeling somewhat confident that, in light of this somber event, we might be mid-truce. As she came through the door, I looked her way and nodded. She walked over, stuck a finger in my face, and said,

"I have a bone to pick with you."

I felt my jaw clench.

Om mani padme hum, om mani padme hum. . . .

This was my latest mantra. Ancient Sanskrit meaning, essentially,

"The road to freedom is lit by compassion."

Om mani padme hum. Om mani padme hum.

A phrase to be repeated, I suppose, till convinced.

I moved away from her to join my brother.

The service was short. The minister kept referring to a scrap of paper in his palm in order to remember Dad's name. There were only a few guests, mostly neighbors. My dad's older brother, my beloved Uncle John and Aunt Barb, had flown in. It was a great comfort to see them, to sit with them. At my father's wife's insistence, I tried at one point to stand and say a few words.

"He was kind, he was a kind man," was about all I managed to repeat in my stupor. "Thank you for coming. Thank you for being here."

"Taps" emanated from silver speakers stuck in the low-hung ceiling. The moment the trumpet sounded, my uncle took my hand. Though it was tinny and prerecorded, like the Muzak at a shopping mall, the melody moved through the room as a sudden transcendence, an eloquent reminder of Dad's service in Tokyo during the Korean conflict. A reminder that he was a man with a history, with chapters and adventures beyond my knowing.

When the service was over, we headed back to the house for a brief reception. I knew I couldn't stay long. Just as I was about to make my escape to the airport, Barbara cornered me on the back patio.

"How dare you," she said, "allow your mother's name to appear in your father's obituary?"

This, I gathered, was the bone she had to pick. A complete surprise, especially as I had not handled the obituary. I had, in fact, handled nothing. I had merely shown up, feeling very much a stranger at my own father's funeral. I responded impulsively.

"What? How dare I? She was the mother of his children."

"Hardly. I did more to raise your little sister and your angry little brother David than she ever—"

"What are you talking about Barbara? And you, you made it so difficult for Dad these last—"

"Oh, you have no idea who we were to each other," she said. "Always treating us like second-class citizens."

"That's not true!" I protested past a stab of guilt.

And so it went. We were perched on the edge of our chairs, the comments flying back and forth, as I tried to get through to her and she to me. I could feel the rage, my left-brain chatter gearing up, saying,

For once in your life, Marty, be strong; give her a piece of your mind!

I half stood. *Off with her freakin' head!* I leaned forward to—I don't know, smack her, throttle her, finally scream in her face? There were these bands of sun across her cheek and I watched my arm reach over and a hand, my hand, suddenly place itself on top of hers.

And everything came to a stop.

A gurgle came from the swimming pool. My heart beat. But the air was perfectly still, electric, and her face emerged. *Barbara.* Her eyes. *Green.*

And we just sat there and beheld each other.

After a long while she squeezed my hand and said,

"I know you lost your daddy today, too. I'm sorry."

"Me too, Barb. I'm sorry."

Barbara's daughter poked her head out to check if we'd drawn blood. When she caught sight of the two of us holding hands, she vanished.

And when I left I kept thinking, I'm still thinking,

What happened?

What in the world was that?

TOMMY AND I WERE on the outskirts of Johannesburg, zooming past vacant lots and former gold mines on our way to a large cheetah preserve. It was our third day together and I was especially excited. This being Africa, I *had* to squeeze in a safari! I'd found out about a large animal preserve not far from the city that offered excursions promising large cats and wild dogs, zebras and ostriches and all manner of wildlife. Since I'd made my reservation for the tour, a vision kept washing over me—a perfect moment tripping upon primordial Africa, a glimpse of a nature-filled Eden.

I'd had good, full days with Tommy. We talked a lot. When I had called ahead from the States to line up a driver (which a friend strongly urged me to do), I'd said to the cheery South African lady from the tourist company, "I was hoping my driver might be someone who grew up in Johannesburg? I mean, who knows personally of the history. I want to have, I guess, a real sense of the . . ."

I fumbled, I recall, because what I was saying, or wanted to say, was that I'd like to be with a black guide. But to come right out with that felt somehow awkward.

"I understand," she'd said. "You don't want to just head off to a safari park. Right? Maybe a township or two, along with your shopping? I know just the guide, someone who will help you have an authentic experience."

I liked Tommy from the moment I met him at baggage claim. He was there holding a sign with my name; it was such a comfort after twenty-two hours of flying. He was low-key and, though we were both timid at first, soon we were talking about his town, his family, his two kids. I loved watching him greet others as we moved through the city, his "Hey, Sister" or "Hey, Bah," his kindly wave, his missing front tooth lending his grin a particular charm.

In our days together I had observed how Tommy's sense of time seemed . . . well, elastic. One morning, when he was taking me around Soweto, he suddenly stopped the van, pulled over to the side of the road, and, without a word, jumped out. I watched as he dashed across the street to a vacant field between two relatively large houses (newer and fancier than the many shacks we had passed). A large pile of apparently unwanted items had been dumped there. Something had caught his eye. He started riffling through stuff as I worked at remaining patient. "When in Rome," I heard myself say. After five or ten minutes he walked back to the van carrying two bound texts the size of Manhattan telephone books. He set them on the dashboard and we took off again. I picked one up. *Basic Computer Languages.* I glanced at the other. *Programming Your Home Computer.*

"You studying computers?" I asked.

"Could be," was all he said. "Could be good."

But on this day, thrilled to be on the way to my mini safari, his mellow sense of time was driving me crazy. We had been nearly two hours on the road and I suspected that we might be lost. When I asked about our direction (which seemed at odds with the one described to me on the phone when I booked the safari) Tommy was tranquility itself. I kept pointing at road signs saying, "Tommy, are you *sure* this is right?" He nodded and said,

"No worries man. That place is by a bridge over a river where my father used to take me."

OK. Go easy, Marty; go with the flow, I told myself. Be the mellow explorer, not the nervous New Yorker. I tried not to look at my watch.

After another quarter of an hour I pointed to another road sign.

"Tommy, I thought maybe . . . um, don't we want to be on the highway much further to the south?" He shrugged.

Fine. What do I know? It's Africa! But sweat was trickling down Tommy's graying sideburns and I couldn't contain my anxiety.

"Look, Tommy, it's *way* late! Let me call the safari place."

"Don't worry, man." Then he opened his phone, "Oh, sorry. Out of minutes."

"What! No phone? Where are we?"

My stomach flipped. *I am going to miss the animals!* And I thought exactly what I'd say to the lady at the tour agency:

"I paid for this driver, this service, so that my trip would be efficient! *Smooth.* This is just crazy, *unacceptable.*"

Finally I spotted a sign indicating our route number, and looking at the map I blurted,

"OK, Tommy. Jesus! This is wrong. *Totally wrong.* Pull over!"

We stopped on the shoulder of the road. It was desolate but for weeds, hills beyond with wildflowers. A Calvin Klein billboard. Tommy turned off the engine and I said,

"Please, *look* at this. OK?"

I scooted toward him and laid the map in his lap. I put my finger where I thought we were and then where we should be.

"See? See Tommy? *Look at this!*" I heard my voice, pinched and piercing. "You're the driver, for God's sake! We're so off path. It says right here. *Look.*"

He was nodding at the map, his nose moving closer but his eyes were sort of darting and . . . it hit me. And I saw him see that it hit me. He didn't know how to read it. I leaned back, folded the map, my chest burning. *Monster.*

There was the wind, the clackety rasp of insects unknown to me.

He stared straight ahead and said,

"You, you people . . . your minds are organized. You see these things. I never got my mind . . . organized."

Just be here, I kept thinking. Oh God, all this busyness, this hunt for sites to be devoured. Just here on the side of a road with Tommy, this gentleman who's told me about his family and shared about his struggles with women, about his father, an important Zulu preacher whom he says he's failed to live up to. This is it. Don't need to be anywhere else, really. *Just here, breathe.*

"Tommy, I'm sorry I . . ."

He stopped me and said,

"You know in school they taught . . ." He grinned for a second. "They taught us to sweep. To mop. To clean shoes properly. Other peoples' shoes."

Open-bed trucks packed with peaches and people rushed by.

"I speak a good English. I used to stay up late listening to a British man on the radio. He had a good voice. I repeated whatever he said, over and over. But I never learned. . . ."

He looked out the window toward the hills. After a long while he said,

"You know, if you listen carefully, the spirits will tell you which plants and flowers will heal you."

Then he said, "Hey. You want us to see my house?"

"Yeah. Sure."

We turned and drove back to town past Soweto, past the church still pocked with bullet holes from the '76 uprising and on toward the township of Alexandra. An explosion of color, a dense collection of houses/shacks, spigots for water at the end of narrow roads. Brightly dressed women sat on crates and on curbs watching as small children scurried in and out from between houses.

We turned and drove down what turned out to be Tommy's street. He told me to roll up my window and lock the door. "And put your camera away. People can be crazy." We stopped at an intersection where a group of young men were standing outside a small corner store. There was a counter with a few fruits and vegetables. They stared at me. I felt every bit the intruding gawker, the tourist who would be off to the airport soon with a computer full of photos and a bag full of souvenirs: carved wood from Soweto, a program from the Market Theater, a book about young Gandhi. We moved past a tight group of shacks. Tommy pointed to one. "It may be an ugly house, but someone beautiful lives inside."

He parked the car behind a cement wall and locked the gate. His neighbor had a sparkling BMW there, next to an outhouse. "That's my privy," Tommy told me. "*With* running water. I'm lucky to have that."

We sat in Tommy's one room divided into two by a hanging blanket, drank a pungent tea. "It is hard to get sleep in the township," he said. "Someone's music, someone's business. You hear it all."

He explained that being a tour guide was a new job for him, part of a government program to get people to work, into new and better kinds of jobs. The tour van was on loan from the

program. He was fortunate to have this house, he said, as it was
sturdier than most. His father had built it. "He was a minister
here. People liked him. He had *many* children. I don't know what
happened to me. I have only two." He laughed and shook his
head. "I didn't get what he got, I guess."

We sipped our tea.

"Can I show you something?" he asked.

We stepped outside past his outhouse onto a side road where
a woman was selling a red-colored fruit. Tommy gestured over
weeds to a shack set back from the road. A broom, half of its
bristles torn away, leaned against the door.

"Look," he said. "When he first came to the city, this is where
he lived. He was a law student then."

I knew instantly who. No matter race, age, or gender, everyone, it seemed, spoke with this tender awe of Mandela. We stood
and stared at the door and Tommy said,

"He came out, after twenty-seven years in prison, and *for-
gave*. It's enough to make you believe."

"In what," I asked. "God?"

Tommy laughed a little and said,

"In *something*. In whatever it is that allowed him to do that.
A man," he said. "A man did that."

ONE EVENING IN SEATTLE a small woman approached me in the lobby of the Intiman Theatre. She was one among an intimate group of folks who'd lingered after the post-play discussion to say good night and offer a few final comments. I noticed her hovering while a tall, Scandinavian-looking gentleman shook my hand with great fervor, saying something along the lines of, "You know, hands down, *anger* is a component of forgiveness. Right? If you don't come to truly understand your own anger, you can't really get to the forgiveness part. They are linked, I believe." I nodded, thinking how sensible that sounded and how elusive that link as my eye kept drifting over to this particular woman. I sensed that she was distressed, somehow. She was, I'd guess, in her mid-forties, with brown hair cut short. She appeared to be alone. When she finally stepped forward, I extended my hand.

"Hello. I'm Martin."

"I know. Rosemarie. I liked the show."

"Thanks."

Her eyes moved from the floor to me and back to the ground. I remained quiet.

"I work with that population," she said.

"Which population?" I asked.

"I . . . I work with men who are . . . I work with 'Bobs.' The ones who do the kind of things he did to you. I work with them in a prison program for offenders. I'm a therapist. I am so sorry what happened to you happened."

"Thanks for your kind words. I'm doing OK." I smiled, conscious of offering evidence of my OK-ness. "Most days, anyway."

"I see that," she said, and smiled back.

"We all have our stuff, God knows."

"Yeah. But, that's a tough one," she said. "I was very moved by your . . . the way you talked of reconciliation. It surprised me. I want to ask you a question."

"Sure."

"Do you think they can be redeemed? I mean, are they beyond redemption?"

"They?"

"Perpetrators."

"No," I said, swiftly and with a certainty that surprised me. And then, in haste, in a jumble, I added, "I mean, I think they are redeemable. They must be. Aren't we all?" The word "redeem" ran amok in in my head. Redeem these coupons for a pair of free shoes! Redeem yourself by volunteering at your local shelter. Buy back, redeem some good grace with some good works, some good old remorse. The nuns, I recalled, used to tell us that without redemption, we'd be condemned to eternal separation from God. The worst possible thing that could happen to a body.

"What they did," she said, "lots of people would call it unforgiveable."

"Doesn't everyone have the chance to be redeemed?"

"Well, you're someone who's been through it," she said. "I couldn't say. I hope so. It's just, I see that some of these people are just plain ill, haunted by their inability to understand or stop their impulses. You can sometimes feel that they're incapable of empathy. It's hard."

"It must be."

"I guess I'm there for a reason." She took my hand. "Thanks for tonight, for what you said. It helped."

She walked away and another woman, older, late sixties, I'd say, touched my shoulder. She spoke softly, in a rather choked whisper:

"Sir, you know that question the lady asked you, about working with those men?"

"Yes."

"Let me ask you. What would you do if you were a parent? A mother? And the victim was your son?"

Her eyes upon me were pure, focused intent.

"I . . . I don't know. I'm not a parent."

"Well, you'd be beyond angry, I can tell you that. You'd want blood."

And off she went.

"I CAN'T SAY I BELIEVE IN GOD, PER SE," he said. "I mean, God is *big* in this town, believe me, but I don't know. Most days I don't know what to make of Him or Her or *it* or whatever. You know?"

"I do," I replied.

I was on my couch in New York thinking what a resonant voice this fast-talking guy had. He was a radio announcer in Salt Lake City. It was midmorning on the East Coast, very early out there in the Rockies. He was about to patch me through by phone to go on the air live for his program. He covered local cultural events and my play was opening there at a small theater, a local actor playing the part of "Marty." This interviewer had read the play and parts of my book and was full of questions.

"I mean, so you believe in God, right?" he asked. "He's all over your book."

I was pulling a loose thread from the hem of my boxer shorts, thinking of getting more coffee.

"Well," I said, "yes, in a manner of speaking . . . I do. God is rather personal, of course. Unnameable. In a way, though, I believe we are all God, part of the Great Spirit. I do consider myself a spiritual seeker."

"Yeah, well you use the word God a lot in your book. Grace and God and all that stuff figures big for you. It seems. You still Catholic?"

"Don't go to church much, no. But that stuff goes in deep when you're young. It's part of who I am, I'd say. I use words like 'God' and 'grace' as a means of expressing a larger reality. I guess."

"Like forgiveness? I mean, man, that's big for you."

"I think about it a lot, yes. Sometimes I think I grasp it, understand it; then I don't. Some days I don't even know how to forgive myself. Lately I've been thinking that forgiveness is basically a flash of nonduality—the realization that we are one. That's all. My enemy and I, you and I . . . *one*."

"Very John Lennon."

"But often it's hard to tap into. Sometimes what I experience is mostly darkness. And self-hate."

"You struggle with that still?"

"From time to time. Yes."

"Ummm, OK. Interesting," he said. "I don't know . . . but let me tell you this. A guy out here, husband, father of two. OK? He was traveling along in his car with his family and a drunk driver—a young guy, hit them. OK? So the man's wife and kids were killed. Terrible, terrible tragedy. Both drivers survived and this man, whose wife and kids were *gone*, I heard him talk on a program about how one day he went to see the young man and the young man's parents and spoke with them. The kid was distraught. I mean, you can imagine, right? So get this, the man said he felt he had to go there and *forgive* this kid! The man who survived the accident said, 'I forgive the young man who crashed into me. I forgive him. I must. The boy is full of remorse, he knows he made a terrible mistake, I forgive him.' Can you freakin' believe that? He said he couldn't go on hating the kid. He had to set the boy free. Himself, too. My God, I just, that moved me so much and I thought, *What is that?* I don't think I could do that. And I was listening to this man who lost so much, I was listening to him thinking he is out of his freakin' mind, you know? But he kept talking and I started to cry. To *cry*, you know? And I thought, OK. I don't believe in God but . . . I don't know . . . I mean, *what is that?*"

And then we went on the air.

I recall nothing about the actual interview.

THE SUMMER OF 2005, NOT LONG AFTER our father's funeral, my brother, Dave, found that he needed, once again, to find a new place and a new way to live. He said so long to Barbara, packed up all that he owned, got into his funky Ford pickup, and headed for the hills.

He drove eastward into the Colorado Rockies and stopped in a little town called Fraser. This small mountain community, known for its warm heart and cold winter, has been dubbed "Icebox of the Nation." A sign is posted near the city limit proclaiming its distinction as the coldest incorporated town in the lower forty-eight states. At 8,550 feet above sea level, Fraser's elevation far exceeds its population of around nine hundred. It's situated adjacent to a popular ski area called Winter Park. One of the peaks the park comprises is a local favorite called "Mary Jane." A place where, in high school days, we loved to smoke a bit of Mary Jane and fly up and down her glorious and bumpy slopes.

After several weeks of camping out in the woods, Dave managed to find a comfortable room for rent in a log cabin with a wonderful housemate, Ingrid, who owned the place. He sounded chipper when he called to tell me where he'd finally landed. This new place sounded promising. He told me about the trees and ever-snowy peaks out his window. The quiet. I was glad for him. Through the years I'd stayed with him in a few of his basement apartments, dank and dimly lit. He once said to me, stamping out a cigarette, "Will I always live like a mole in a hole?"

I read a passage about these early days in Fraser in one of Dave's notebooks.

> *My soul belongs in the mountains. The happiness and intrinsic sense of self (is this what I would call it?) is here.*
>
> *A Mountain vista view! Fitting, as I am starting over, that I should start with a new notebook to record my thoughts. I'm excited, actually excited for the first time in a long time! With a roof over my head I can now start the process of looking for work. I still haven't the foggiest what I will do.*

He managed to find all sorts of employment. In the warmer months he took shifts at a lumberyard and year-round he waited tables at a popular local restaurant called Deno's. Eventually, he got a great job supervising the computer room at the local elementary school. He became the very popular "Mr. Moran, IT Guy." I stopped into his classroom on one of my visits west, enchanted to see the way the kids flocked around him. "Mr. Moran? Mr. Moran, how do I print out this map?" I watched as they raised their palms to receive a high-five whenever they solved a thorny problem, saw how he made them laugh even as he was playing tough: "I will bite your fingers off if you eat food near your computer!"

He also volunteered at the National Sports Center for the Disabled teaching handicapped kids to ski. Turned out he had a special gift for working with autistic children, and on weekends, he often led young blind skiers down the slopes. His life seemed to jell in the Icebox of the Nation.

He'd convinced me to fly out to see him the first winter he was there. He said the snow was great and that we'd hit the slopes like when we were kids. We ended up hanging out a lot in one of his favorite bars. He'd raise his fresh pint of Guinness: "You see, Mart—this is a drinking town with a skiing problem!" And before he took his first sip of beer, he would stick his index finger into the foam and draw a smiley face there—scoop for the mouth, dot dot for the eyes—every time, without fail. Only then would he bring the glass to his lips and drink, leaving his mustache laced with foam and a wide grin beaming from amid his bushy beard.

This entry in his journal was dated 7/28/2005, five weeks after our father died, soon after he found his new digs.

Another day blossoms, flowers rising and shining opening their petals to let the comfort of the sun's rays in. The Rocky Mountain chickadees performing a concerto, strategically positioned in the grove of lodge pole pines, chirping in such harmony you can't help but stop and listen. Just what they are performing only they know . . . nature's music.

And I sit, wanting nothing more than to listen, to listen to the sounds, the wind's rustling the branches of the aspen, ponderosa pine, lodge pole pine, Douglas fir. Waving the grasses to and fro: Now on nature's radio . . . coming right up. The river's clap . . . bumble bee's buzz with fly by appearance by the clicking cricket, the clackety crow.

We're so disillusioned by our lives. There is a cure—listen, listen and allow nature to quiet the mind to hold you in her hand and cover your being with the sights, sounds, smells, textures and tastes. Breathe. This is where we belong.

THE CONFERENCE PACKET HAD SAID something about free continental breakfast. The thought of coffee and carbs pried me from bed. The room was cold, the AC blasting. I pulled opened the curtains. That's when I remembered that I'd been given a room on a high floor. I'd arrived from the airport the night before. Out the hotel window, as far as I could see, was desert, bright heat, sweeping freeways. This large and spanking-new complex—hotel, shops, and restaurants—was plunked on the outskirts of the city. Beyond it was a landscape one might find on the moon. Not a human body in sight.

I tried several times and ways to pry open the window. Sealed shut, apparently. I was longing for air, the unconditioned kind, and so called the front desk. What followed was a brief and rather frustrating discussion about suicide prevention, environmental economy, and tamper-proof windows.

The mini fridge gave a sucking sound as I pulled the door open. I grabbed a bottle of water, cracked open the plastic lid, and drank as I gazed again out toward the terrain where tribes with names like Hopi and Ak-Chin and Cocopah once lived. Where they'd invented, in fact, a vast and ingenious irrigation system that allowed them to thrive for generations on this arid land.

I slipped on some clothes, stuck my baseball cap over unruly hair, found the plastic card key, and headed out and down the hall—a brash swirl of orange carpet and bright lights. A cart full of cleaning equipment stacked with rolls of toilet paper and folded towels stood near the elevator. Other than this, still no sign of human bodies. I pushed the elevator button. The cube opened, accompanied by the sound of two meditative dings. A feminine voice cooed from the beyond,

"Going down."

"Yes," I replied to the great spirit, "down to Earth please."

There were many, many large meeting rooms with names like the Prince Edward, the Sir Drake, the Lady Grey, and Hall A and Hall B, and other handmade signs with arrows indicating which rooms had which conference events. I reached the main hall. It was the size of a football field. Or so it seemed. Folks were busy opening up the many display tables and booths that circled the huge space. A long counter with coffee and bagels was placed in the middle of the room. I filled a Styrofoam cup, found a moist bagel and a tiny tub of Philadelphia cream cheese, and moved to a seat at one of the big, round tables.

I gazed around the room and, OK, it's a cliché, but *I could not believe my eyes.* I was aware that it was a convention for sex therapists but my God! Stalls meant to educate, elucidate, and lubricate human intercourse had popped up everywhere. "Contraception," "Viagra," "Gender Bend." Not fifteen feet away, a middle-aged woman who could have been a PTA mom was demonstrating a contraption that had two seats gliding upward and down and back and forth like a little seesaw. She was pointing out various aspects of the ride to an interested customer, another older lady. They were both focused particularly on the two gleaming dildos strategically mounted, one rising from each seat. A bicycle built for two. Leaving my coffee for a moment, I got up and moved closer. By then the saleswoman was filling out a purchase order for the "Monkey Rocker," while explaining that, yes, you can certainly sit in either direction for anal or vaginal penetration. And, yes, the dildos are adjustable and available in various sizes. The frankness of the transaction was rather stunning. The frankness of filling holes, filling needs.

I glanced around at a few more of the teeming tables, replete with gels and toys and pamphlets and people. At times, I found myself averting my eyes like a shy kid. I'm a fifty-year-old gay guy living in New York City. Why was I reacting like a parochial prude? It was as if I was back at Christ the King Elementary. I ambled about timid and titillated. That such a conference existed, that all these professional folks were chatting with the greatest of ease about sex was a rather fabulous surprise. And all so early in the morning.

I returned to my table. A man sat down across from me. His floppy paper plate was stacked with bagels and chunks of honeydew. We nodded at each other.

"Good morning."

"Morning."

Where are you from?" he asked.

"New York"

"Milwaukee."

"Ahh."

There we sat in the great hall, floating in a sea of sexual education, surrounded by a panoply of grown-up paraphernalia, chitchatting. We exchanged some basics. He was a therapist and I explained that that I was an actor there to perform a one-man play I'd written.

"Oh, that's the sex abuse play, right?" he asked.

I cringed and stopped myself from launching into an explanation of the play being oh so much more than *that*. Hunched over our weak coffee, clutching our plastic knives, fraternally spreading our Philadelphia cheese, I replied,

"Um, yes. That play."

Then he asked,

"You going to go to the dungeon?"

"Excuse me?"

"There's a field trip to the dungeon Saturday night."

"A dungeon?"

"Yes. The local BDSM community has invited any therapists who would like to, to come and observe an evening session at their dungeon."

"Seriously?"

"Yes. Saturday night. Everyone's talking about it. Space is limited. You should sign up."

Before heading back to my room to shower, with a curious quickening of the blood, I made my way to the appropriate desk. There was a sign welcoming one and all to come and observe the local "Power-Exchange" group. Two exceedingly friendly ladies were manning the table and they explained that a bus had been hired for those who signed up. That there were still spots available. They handed me a clipboard with a couple of forms requiring my signature—a safety waiver of some sort, a confidentiality agreement. I didn't pay much mind. I was excited, a bit scared. It was like signing up for a raft trip, a tour of the Grand Canyon. I scribbled my name and handed the forms back. One of the gals smiled and said,

"The kink community looks forward to hosting you."

"The kinks invite the shrinks," I said.

We all laughed.

If you Google the word "kink," the first two items that show up are a British rock group and a rare dialect of Japanese.

"Hey, Tiger, get that *kink* out the hose, would you?"

The voice is my father's, floating across the dry heat of a summer day. His request, as best I can recall, was my first encounter with the word kink. His face is still young and vivid to me, the handsome reporter on his weekend off from the *News*, a cigarette dangling from his lips. He's just mowed his beloved lawn, the grass clippings are bagged, and soon we'll stuff them into the back of our Plymouth station wagon and take them to the dump. After, we'll stop at McDonald's for double cheeseburgers. A Saturday afternoon in the backyard of our Denver home in the brand-new and modest suburb called Virginia Vale. A small grid of alphabetized streets—Dahlia, Dexter, Elm, Eudora—with single-story, shoebox-shaped houses. The trees are all saplings, most of the families young. First-time owners. It's the sixties.

"Hey, Tiger, get that *kink* out, would you?"

It's a sun-drenched scene. Our freshly groomed lawn is a deep shade of green, the Rocky Mountain sky a hard, high blue. The hose is pinched and I run to unfold it as Dad sets the sprinkler. That crazy kind of sprinkler that hisses and spins in anxious circles, spurting and clicking as if working out its own twisted self. There are grass stains at the knees of Dad's long-legged khakis. He's not one for shorts, not one for exposure. Wisps of hair peek out from the upper button of his buttoned-down shirt. His is a body encased, unknown to me. He's sealed away somehow and I'm dimly aware of a longing—does he feel it, too?—hanging hidden between us in the mile-high air. An ache to know and be known, to link with the larger, the more powerful person over there across the grass.

Get the crick out, would you? The bend, the knot, the crazy curve that folds in on itself and I wonder, I do, does all this writing come down to an effort to get the kink out? A spiritual, philosophical, a physical kink?

On the way to the dungeon that hot Saturday night, vague images gleaned from vague sources popped willy-nilly into my head. Medieval castles I'd seen in Europe, chambers where prisoners were chained to brick walls; damp basements with damsels in distress, wrists wrapped in ropes; armor and axes and instruments of torture. A scene from a film: a tall woman in leather boots brandishing a nasty whip, a man in boxers, his hands bound to the bedposts. The famous critic Kenneth Tynan's diaries, the dress-up scenes, the role-playing depicted therein of a few famous "twisted" Brits.

I realized I had no real idea of what I might be about to see.

The parking lot was enormous, as were most of the buildings in this industrial sector of the town. A tall man in blue jeans and cowboy boots was directing folks to the appropriate parking places. He greeted us with a wave as we walked toward the venue.

His nametag read, "Master John"

It occurred to me that Master might be a misspelling of Mister but upon entering the premises I spotted many more nametags affixed on the shirts of friendly fellows (and women, too)—Master Greg and Master Steve among them. And most of the tags included a one- or two-word designation printed below the name.

Bondage.
Discipline.

Leather Boy.
Submission.
Military.
Dominatrix.

These categories, we were later told, were displayed for our benefit, so that if we had any questions about a specific proclivity, we could address the appropriate person.

The main room was enormous with very high ceilings. You could look up and see second and third levels, open, loftlike spaces.

Folding chairs had been set up on the perimeter of the main floor. We filed in and quietly took our seats. My body, my blood was pumping—anticipation of all sorts. At the prospect of seeing human nakedness, not just exposed flesh but unmasked desire. I was frightened, too, about the possibility of witnessing pain. Suffering in conjunction with the erotic? I'd wished I had more experience or knowledge of this world. In the early eighties (just pre-AIDS) I visited a notorious New York City gay club, its basement known as a sexual free-for-all. I well recall descending the steps into darker regions. Through the dim light I glimpsed hammocks and slings and bodies enmeshed. I climbed right back up the stairs to the main bar and dance floor. Too scared to explore.

As I folded my nervous self into my little folding chair, I felt utterly privileged, amazed, and terrified at this opportunity to have a sort of sanctioned escort down into the basement.

A middle-aged man with long black hair came forward to a standing microphone. He looked to be, perhaps, Native American. His voice was lovely, his words laced with an intoxicating cadence that I could not pinpoint. Spanish? Mexican?

"We all want to welcome you. We want to thank you for coming and we want you to feel safe and taken care of. That's how it is here. It's a safe place and we take care of one another."

He spoke a bit about himself: his work in education, his part-time job at a local ranch. I was struck by his eloquence and humor. His manner was calm, his presence authentic and grounded. He talked about the reason, the importance, for this evening's event. As best as I can recall, he said something like this:

"We are here to show you, to share with you in the mental health industry, who we are. We are teachers and lawyers and ranchers, just plain folk from all walks of life and we comprise what we lovingly call our Kink Community. Again, we welcome you. It is our aim to help you understand what might be your prejudice about our community and communities like ours. Some of your own clients back home may well be part of their own kink community and we hope that you don't automatically think of us, of them, as someone with a disorder. For many of us, our exploration of power dynamics and BDSM is our path to a deeper connection. It is simply a part of who we are and we feel open and healthy about it. Perhaps tonight we can dispel some fears or biases. You'll notice that we've all worn nametags so that you can identify us by name and ask any questions related to what we are into. We are here to answer your questions openly and honestly. Once the demonstration is over, please feel free to stay and we can all talk. We brought some goodies, refreshments, our friend Fred's famous meatballs, fruit salad and other treats. We've put together a nice potluck. And remember: if at any time you feel unsafe or uncomfortable, just know that you are free to step out. There's coffee and tea in the lobby."

So civilized.

As couples began to enter and take their places at the various stations, a kind of master of ceremonies entered and wandered about the space. A silent figure, a sort of ringmaster bearing witness and a kind of authority. It had been explained that his role was to be sure that no one was going too far and that no one was in any real danger of being hurt. He was a big guy with bright eyes and an enormous gut. He wore a dark vest and had a bushy beard. He made me think of the MC in the Broadway musical *Cabaret.* In fact, the whole event was very theatrical. Two-person scenes were now unfolding, being played out in various areas. It was as if we'd been invited to a rehearsal, a performance-art piece. This felt familiar to me. We were an audience watching a show. We'd been given permission to be voyeurs, peeking at human improvisation.

Directly across from me, a tall man wearing leather pants and boots began flogging a woman. Her bare backside, cellulite and all, was facing a large web of ropes to which she was fastened. He whipped slowly, with long pauses between his careful lashes. Sometimes when he'd pause, he would walk up and whisper into her ear. Her back became red. A small cut appeared, a tiny dash of blood. My mirror neurons, the ones said to be responsible for empathy, were firing. I considered (for a moment) stepping out. But, no, I hunched forward, crossed my legs, all kinked up in my little chair, a bundle of sensations.

A Saint Anthony's Cross, or Tau Cross, as it is also known, was set up in the far left corner of the space. The cross, shaped like the letter T, was named for the fourth-century Egyptian hermit. A naked woman was bound to it and a tall guy wielded an instrument, a contraption that appeared to electrocute or sting her. I couldn't tell what it was. Mostly I averted my eyes. Whatever this power exchange was, it spooked me.

As I looked around, I began to realize how all this, of course, was deeply familiar. From the time I could walk, I had grown up seeing images, portraits, sculptures, frescoes of all those beautiful, sexy, tortured saints. The ropes, the arrows, the suffering, the flesh, the flames. All of it bound up, in one way or another, with the sacred, the sacrificial, the transcendent. Bound up with spirit trumping the body, reaching through pain toward God for the sake of the soul. Here it was in all its Catholic Technicolor.

In the distance hanging from a long cord, a woman was enfolded in a sheet and bound round with several ropes. Or perhaps the same rope wrapped several times. She looked as though she was swathed in a cocoon. She dangled there as a redheaded lady poked and prodded her, rocked the cocoon, tightened and loosened the ropes so that the hidden body rose and fell a few delicate inches at a time. Her face was obscured, but a shank of her silver hair was exposed, draping toward the ground. I am not sure what was really going on, what the actual exchange was, but it was fascinating to witness this suspension of body, the intimacy of the interchange between the two women. They were lost utterly, it seemed, in their silent, subtle interaction.

There was a table over to my right that looked just like a massage table but wider, larger. Next to it was a counter filled with equipment, instruments: a large lighter, lighter fluid, white gloves, several cup-shaped domes of glass, small rods and tuning forks tapered into phallic shapes. A woman was lying on the table facedown. A big guy, dressed all in leather, stood over her. He looked like some sort of severe centurion. He very carefully and systematically put on gloves, heated the cup-shaped glass with flames, and then slowly, methodically, placed the hot glass in various spots along her back and buttocks and legs.

Meanwhile, directly in front of where we were sitting, a two-character play was unfolding. A young woman in a plaid skirt and knee-high socks was facing off with a very strict older lady who wore a prim uniform and held a small whip. (Miss Jean Brodie!) This seemed a classic S&M scenario, almost a joke. But their improvisation was clearly very serious and alive. We were very close to the two "actors" and I admired their focused bravery.

"Have you been bad?" "What did you do?" "Get down when I speak to you!! Bend over. Now!"

At moments we laughed. The repetitive lines were sometimes funny and this made for safer, easier viewing than most of the other power-exchange stations. I wondered what this would be like on a night where seventy-five shrinks were *not* watching, on a regular evening when they had more privacy. (Perhaps there would have been some men as naked and submissive as the women?) In any case, the schoolgirl and her disciplinarian carried on like troopers: skirt pulled down, bottom spanked. It occurred to me that Heisenberg's uncertainty principle must be in play here, that we observers could not help but alter the goings-on in some way. It did seem, though, that observation was an essential element for this group; that being witnessed was a part of the experience of the dungeon, whether visiting therapists were present or not. And that moved me. That such private exploration and intimacy was there to be shared, witnessed.

The biggest surprise, and most poignant for me, was what unfolded next.

After an hour or so, things began to wind down. The dominators tenderly guided their partners away from the intensity of the action. The couples moved together, gingerly, toward the floor. And there they quietly, meditatively embraced. Cuddled.

I noticed the man who had been flogging place, ever so gingerly, a bit of balm and a Band-Aid where the streak of blood had appeared on his partner's back. It was like a sweet dance of amends. Of forgiveness? For the wanting, for the doing? I found myself tearing up. The man who had initially welcomed us had told us that this would be an important aspect of the evening. It was known as aftercare.

The room was silent. The MC was standing above us, on a perch, serenely beholding this calm choreography of reconciliation. I was imagining the possible whispered conversations, the words across the silence: "Are you all right?" "I am, yes. Thank you for that exquisite connection, for that just-enough pain. For you, for holding me just tight enough, hurting me just this much. Rest now. Rest in peace."

I had no idea, of course, what, if anything, was being said. There well may have been exchanges of reproach. But it was so serene. The place felt bathed in . . . love. Imagine the deep understanding, the negotiating, the trust to work out a threshold of pleasure and pain. It would have to be, I imagined, highly conscious communication. Wouldn't you think? It all struck me as an extremely aware, a deeply mindful experience. I admired it. Was so moved by it.

Over homemade meatballs and potato salad, ginger snaps and soda pop, we all stood under the brighter light of the lounge and kitchen area as we mingled and chatted. It felt awkward at first. The couples who had "performed," as well as many other members of the dungeon who hadn't, stood around or sat about on couches and perched on windowsills. Several were helping to serve food and drinks. The atmosphere was one of quiet celebration, it seemed. There was a tender vulnerability in the air. After much thought and planning, they had "come out" to a large group of mental health professionals, and here it was; they'd pulled it off.

There was a young man standing alone just beyond the potluck tables. *Discipline* was writ upon his nametag. He was, I'd say, late twenties. He was among the youngest of the community, or so he appeared to me. Hands in pockets, baggie khakis, seemingly shy, he and his tag aroused my attention. There had been no men among the "acted upon" and I admit that disappointed me. I stepped toward the young man, introduced myself, and asked him if he could help me with what exactly he meant by his moniker. He immediately obliged. He talked with great intensity of his need and love for a man who had come into his life through this community. The man, he told me, was a high-ranking military officer. He spoke of this officer with awe, as you would a commander, a beloved teacher. He told me that for the most part their relationship was long distance. That was why his master was not in attendance; he was stationed in another state. But they spoke nearly every morning by phone, and his man had extremely strict rules about what he could eat, about the amount of daily exercise—pull-ups, push-ups—he *must* do. "Oh, he makes me work, sweat. I *have* to do it. Drive myself, or else."

"Or else?" I asked.

"Oh, I don't even want to say. He yells at me, man. He spanks me, you know, in a way, over the phone. Sometimes in person. I would not be achieving what I am in my life if I did not have his push. His care."

I saw then that I was viewing this conversation, the whole evening, through a kind of Masters and Johnson lens. You know: attraction, sex, orgasm, cigarette. Consequently, I asked the young man, naively, "Well, is there . . . I mean: do you have . . . sex together?" And he looked at me rather uncomprehending, it seemed, as if to say, man you are way off base, and simply said, "No, it's not about *that* really; it's much more. . . . I don't know the words but—" Our conversation was interrupted by another of the therapists. I left it at that.

I often think of the young man's nonplussed reaction to my question about sex. It keyed me in, opened my mind to begin to see that the roles, partnerships, relationships were of a much more complex and mysterious nature than I had ever imagined. I could feel my heart, my body stirred toward possibility. Could I be so brave as to embark on such an exploration of desire, of need, if it presented itself so strongly?

I turned and saw the man who was the "fire" guy, the one with the massage table, and I walked over and spoke to him. He had seemed so imposing and frightening to me in performance, but the second I approached him, I was struck by his open face, his puppy-dog eyes. He could not have been gentler or more direct in answering my questions.

"I teach history at a local college," he explained. "I do some body work and alternative medicine."

"It looked dangerous what you were doing. Does it scar the skin?"

"No. Not if you're careful. Not if you know what you're doing. Heat is a most powerful sensation when used correctly. You can work with the most sensitive parts of the body."

By the time we got done speaking he had described to me how it's possible to place the heated glass on the tip of the penis or near the vulva. He showed me the tuning fork with the phallic shape and explained how it can be inserted anally or vaginally. He struck it and told me to hold it a moment, to feel the deep vibration. The human imagination is wondrous.

The flogging couple was standing near, arm in arm. I asked her if it hurt. She shook her head. I patted her shoulder in a gesture of thanks. She looked a bit surprised at my touch. Was it OK, I asked, that I had touched her? "I don't know," she said, turning to her partner (her master, I supposed). "Ask him if it's OK."

He nodded and I patted her shoulder gently, once again, and thanked them.

Before I left I ended up speaking for a few moments to the woman with the shank of gray hair who had been hanging from the ceiling in bondage. She showed me the rope burns on her arms and indicated that she had some on her legs and backside as well. There were red streaks that she said would turn to bluer bruises within a day or so.

"Wow," I said, with obvious concern.

"Oh, it's nothing," she said. "The bruises disappear pretty quickly." She turned to the redhead who'd been her partner and said, "She is absolutely the best. She *knows* exactly what she's doing. It was really, really great tonight. She's exquisite."

"What . . . what do you feel?" I asked, not knowing what to ask or what I wanted to ask. "I mean . . . is there a lot of pain?"

"Well, there's pain but . . ." she smiled at me and then looked at her partner. "There's some kind of endorphin release and all sorts of sensations. Pleasure. Falling into, surrendering to her, to gravity, to trust. I am so in myself, my body, but, then, the communication is so intense, so in the moment and I feel then that I leave my body, I float, beyond, to a place where everything just flows. It's a kind of exercise and when it's good, and she is good, I . . . transcend."

"Transcend what, would you say?" I asked.

"The self," she said.

There was a Master once who said:

To study the way is to study the self.
To study the self is to forget the self.
To forget the self is to allow the ten thousand things to flow.

—Zen Master Dogen, (1200–1253), from the "Genjokoan"

DAVE AND I WERE WALKING ON A ROAD near his cabin in Fraser. This was the third, maybe the fourth time I'd traveled there. We'd just had dinner and were in good spirits. There were often long silences between us, months sometimes without a word or a call, but when we'd find each other again after a year or sometimes two, there was usually a burst of joy and my sweet brother, who could be so somber and silent, would open like a book full of secret tales.

"So, yeah, I was on my way to the doctors," he was saying. "I had an appointment down in Denver. I made good time on the trip down to the city, so I decided to stop at REI. You know, that big sports store?"

A bright moon lit the dirt road where we walked. It was early spring; patches of snow were still scattered about and gleaming at the bases of pine trees. There was a wild racket of what I thought were crickets emanating from the woods. Dave walked slowly, cigarette in hand, occasionally scratching his thick beard between puffs.

"You remember how big that store is? They have lots of great gear. I wanted to look at maybe getting a new sleeping bag. Anyway, I parked in the lot and got out of the truck and started to walk toward the store when suddenly I knew something was wrong. Really wrong. I felt a pain, a kind of rough thud in my chest and a weird feeling in my arm, and I got right away what was up. I turned around to get back in the truck to drive myself to the emergency room. I wasn't that far from Denver General. Well, damn if I hadn't left my keys in the ignition. And, of course, it was locked. Too little blood was going to the brain, I guess. So

I had to crawl through the back of the truck and then through the rear window of the cab. I squeezed in—I'd done this before—and started the damn thing and drove to the hospital. There were parking places on the street, I probably should have pulled over right there but I knew if I didn't die I'd be in there for a while and so I'd better get to the long-term parking garage."

"You're kidding me," I said.

"Nope."

"I can't believe your presence of mind!"

"Presence of poverty, man. I hated the thought that if I came out alive my truck would be towed and I'd have a whopping ticket. Too much to bear, man."

"Why didn't you call someone?"

He took a drag from his Marlboro. Gave me a quick grin, bright and sharp in the lunar light.

"So," he continued, "I parked and walked into emergency and said to the nurse, 'Hi, I'm having a heart attack.'"

"How did she know to take you seriously?"

"Oh, she knew. She *knew* that I knew. I must have looked like hell. I flashed my MedicAlert bracelet and, you know, I *know* hospitals. I gave her my basic info and in like seconds they had me on a table in some side room and I remember the fluorescent lights and commotion but, next thing I knew, I woke up with this stint in my heart."

"Stint?"

"Stent," I guess. "After a short stint in Denver General."

"It sounds harrowing."

"I don't know. Par for the course," he said and shrugged.

"You ever call anyone?"

"Not till after it all happened."

"Jesus, Dave," I said.

I sipped the last of my Sierra Nevada Pale Ale as we trudged along. Dave always made sure to have some in his fridge when I came to visit. He knew it was my favorite. A sweet host, he was unfailingly thoughtful about certain things. Every Christmas, gifts for each member of our family would appear through the post—good coffee, books of photography, poetry—carefully wrapped with handwritten notes tucked within.

We walked north on Crooked Creek Road, the insistent singing rising from the woods and ponds around us. All was quiet but for the crunch of our steps. I was trying to imagine life in his shoes. Trying to envisage driving myself to the emergency room while knowing I was having a heart attack. Parking the truck, talking to the nurse. What was it like, little brother, to be negotiating all of this alone? Alone. I was trying to think in what world, in what life, this kind of health crisis would be an expected occurrence, part of an ongoing possibility or routine. By the time he was thirty he had been in and out of the hospital at least a dozen times.

His diabetes was diagnosed when he was six or seven. Mom was upset to find that he'd wet his bed yet again and, finally, a trip to the doctor revealed that his pancreas had fallen down on the job. Now, in his early forties, his skin had red marks from the prick of so many tests taken, shots given.

He had to contend with getting compared with me, I figured. The older brother who went off to Stanford, the basically healthy bio son to Dave's adopted self. Or perhaps I was creating some script that had more to do with my own ego. But I was thinking it as we walked together, as I tried to comprehend his trials. As I tried to be a good brother.

"Yeah, those fucking nurses and doctors were fast, once I got there," he said. "They saved me. Saved me for now, anyway, but. . . ."

"But what?"

He shrugged and took another deep suck off his Marlboro. I winced. (*Like a match to gasoline*, my dear friend Ken, a doctor, had said to me when I asked him about Dave's diabetes and cigarettes.)

"But what?" I asked again.

"Well, the writing is on the wall, man."

He looked to the sky, the milky sky, and blew a stream of smoke.

"That line is from some Old Testament story, isn't it?" I asked.

"Sounds about right," Dave said.

We walked. On the far side of the wide meadow before us, across the train tracks where Union Pacific cars clattered and whistled their way through the valley several times a day, the craggy wall of the Continental Divide rose up. "Granite Backbone of the Country," Steinbeck called it. It was etched against the star-filled sky. The Big Dipper and Polaris hung right there before us, clear as bells. At one point Dave swept his cigarette from one end of the valley to the other and said,

"This place, you see, bro, this place is just one big hug from God."

"The crickets are singing like mad," I said.

"Oh, that's the hum of love you're hearing, brother. Not crickets but little frogs. Wood frogs. Peepers."

"Peepers?"

"Yep. It's spring. They *know.* Slightest rise in temp and they rise from the dead. Literally. They're basically frozen all winter. They can stop their heartbeat for weeks at a time. Bizarre, huh? They have some kind of internal antifreeze and hang out there more dead than alive just below the surface but come spring, it takes them like a day to defrost. And guess what's on their mind?"

"Well . . . ?"

"Yup. Hooking up. That's what the racket is. They wake up looking for love," he said, sounding like the sweet philosopher he often was. "I guess we all have that in common."

"You got anyone right now?"

He shrugged. "There was a girl from Granby but. . . . nah. She was crazy. Not anyone. Not now."

We walked. And walked.

"Look," he said.

"What?"

"Just this, dude."

He pointed to his foot as he stepped forward. His white sneaker glowed. "Look," he said as he took another step. "It's all we can do." His legs moved with a kind of measured pace now, as if willing time to slacken. "And this . . ." he said again as his foot crunched on the gravel and lifted. "It's all there is." He took a step. And another. "All we can do is—be *here.*" He moved forward again. "And here," he repeated. "And here. And here . . ."

His voice trailed off as we walked northward, side by side in the glow of night, encircled by the insistent song of want.

LA REPETITION.

That's French for rehearsal.

The repetition.

I dig for the root. One text indicates it's from Middle French: *Rehercier. To re harrow; re dig.* To turn over, as with soil or ground. To cultivate. You'll also find: to go over, to review, to train, to repeat. To practice. Like kung fu. Which, loosely translated, means daily practice of a skill that takes a hell of a lot of patience. And effort.

We practice, repeat, until we get it good and right.

In my working life, to rehearse a play is to assume that you are aiming toward an ultimate goal, an end point at which you feel ready to be *seen.* You are rehearsing your way toward . . . presence. Perfection? Toward opening.

The camera rolls or, more often for me, *opening night* arrives. The clock strikes eight, you take a deep breath and pray that the character you've created and the story you offer is complete. At least complete enough that you don't feel too bad about charging admission.

What if it's always a rehearsal and never a done deal?

"Your practice is never over," say the Zen Buddhists about meditation.

An actor I know often says the same thing. "Rehearsal is never finished; there's no such thing as perfect. I get freaked out thinking I have to be 'absolutely right.' The premiere isn't a finished project, a performance is never *frozen.* It is ever-changing, ongoing, an unfolding. It's more fun that way, don't you think? It's always a rehearsal."

The many things we practice. Law. Yoga. Medicine. Meditation. Dentistry. Baseball. Massage. Fencing. Fucking. Kissing. Religion. Writing. Loving. Forgiving. Violin. Marriage.

Compassion.

Gertrude Stein called life itself,

"The hymn of repetition."

THE LAST TIME I visited David in Colorado was in March of 2009. I'd flown to Denver in order to see my high school friend Ken. Ken, at age forty-nine, a successful doctor and father of three, was battling his way through the final stages of colon cancer. I slept in his guest room for a few nights, celebrated Passover with all his wonderful family, and then headed up over Berthoud Pass and into Fraser. I was shaken from seeing, from essentially saying so long, to my pal Ken, whom I loved so dearly. I felt some measure of solace as I ascended into the quiet of the mountains and passed Mary Jane, where Ken and I and our closest school chums had often skied away our young Saturdays.

The spring melt was beginning and the busy season winding down. Dave took time off work so we could hit the slopes. He pulled out his Telemark skis that first day and finagled a deal for me to get ski equipment rent-free. Handing me a six-pack of Corona he mumbled, "Bring this around the back door of the shop; ask for Jeff. He'll fix you up."

I trailed behind Dave, feeling my knees, my age, the altitude. Dave flew down the trails. He'd become a fluid and versatile skier. I loved watching him bounce around the moguls, turning and soaring with his fierce athletic grace.

It was the third day that I was there and, as if on some unspoken cue, things fell apart. I was at the window buying a lift ticket. The guy in the ticket booth, like so many young men employed at the ski areas, was handsome and Huckleberry Finn friendly, a ski bum with a tanned face and a dazzling smile. I asked the guy for help, half joking, as I was having trouble affixing the ticket to my jacket's zipper—a snazzy down coat that I'd borrowed from ever-fashionable Dave. After my dawdling at the window, I walked to where my baby brother was putting on his skis.

"Couldn't figure out how to put this dang thing on," I said.

"You're like a fucking child!" he snapped and skied off toward the lift.

And that was it.

The door closed, my tenderhearted brother's tight-lipped fury took center stage, and I took a deep breath. We'd all been counseled about the mood swings, the blood sugar levels. I knew he was besieged with medical issues and nutrition complications and had recently seen a psychopharmacologist for help with his depression. His trials were many and ongoing. When we were younger—Dave in his mid-teens, me early twenties—he had opened up to me a few times about his deep sadness and suicidal feelings. I was able to speak of my own battle with suicide. We sat quietly in his room; I rubbed his back till he fell asleep. I think I was able to comfort him. Now, I didn't know how to get in, how to help him with all he'd been handed. And what moved through me that day, I recall, along with my abiding sense of having somehow let him down, was a desire to slap him.

"Dave?" I called out. "I'm sorry I kept you waiting!" He kept gliding away and so we moved to our separate corners. Eventually we skied separate slopes.

It was *so* frustrating. This often seemed to happen. A moment would arrive, forty-eight or seventy-two hours into a visit, when the glow of reunion wore off and things went sour. I couldn't put my finger on it—was it simply who I was or who we were together? Whatever the reason, here it was again, the dark cloud clamping down and cutting us off.

When Dave and I were together, people would often comment about how much we looked alike. We'd always smile at each other when this happened. It was cool. Our secret. If we chose to share that Dave was adopted, people would be genuinely amazed. It pleased me because Dave was handsome and sweet. I hoped it pleased him, too. We were true brothers, if not by nature, then by nurture. That's what I felt, believed. I always hoped and trusted that Dave knew I was no less his kin for being born of different parents. But, if I'm honest, must I not admit that the question of blood floated somewhere in the air? Undermining, perhaps, the certainty of our bond?

I spoke about this not long ago with my younger sister, Carolyn, who's also adopted. She told me that she and Dave always shared the deepest link of all: their sense of distance, of being one step removed, from the family. "How could we not, Mart? It's just the truth. We come from somewhere else."

"But Mom and Dad brought you home to us when you were only two weeks old. You're like flesh and blood."

"It is what it is," she said. "You can't know what it's like. We always felt different. Separate."

On the final night of that March visit, Dave and I strolled not far from his cabin to have dinner outdoors. Dave kneeled, grilling chicken over a small fire. The Indian Peeks were visible just beyond where we crouched. His Marlboro dangled from the corner of his mouth. One eye shut against the smoke curling toward his face, looking so much in that moment like our father it startled me. I watched him, touched by his effort, his concentration on making our dinner. He liked to cook; he was good at it.

Under his mountain man beard I could still see the baby face of the paperboy who sold more *Denver Post* subscriptions than any other delivery boy in our neighborhood. His adorable ten-year-old mug had appeared in the *Post*—braces across his big front teeth, the glimmering grin of the winner of the sales contest, a trip to Disneyworld. I saw the sweet kid who mowed the lawn and took out the trash; the youngest of our brood, the one I knew bore the deepest brunt of our parents' unhappy split. I sipped my beer. His eyes still wouldn't meet mine as he flipped the chicken, flicked an ash.

I made a stab into the silence.

"Hey, Dave, is that Devil's Thumb up there?"

"Yep." His lips were pursed, his face grim.

"Have you climbed it?"

"Yep."

We sat and ate in silence, chewing our chicken. Then he turned and said,

"You know, I figure forgiveness is the way to the sacred self."

OK, I was thinking, did I hear that right?

We were quiet for a time and then I asked,

"What do you mean, Dave? What do you have to forgive?"

He lit up yet another Marlboro. Gave a shrug.

More silence.

"Dave, can I ask you something? You seem *so* angry. What are you angry about?"

And after a moment he said,

"Betrayal, I guess."

"Betrayed by what, by who?"

"By birth," he said. He gave a flicker of a grin and, then, all in a rush,

"My body is like an enemy, you know? This diabetes. And the way it all happened, so . . . random. Handed off like a package, adopted by Mom and Dad, who had no business raising kids."

"Well, they did their best, I guess. I know it must have been . . ."

"You can't *know!*" he exploded. "You left the house when I was eleven. You don't know what I've lived!" He glared up toward Devil's Thumb.

"Dave?"

He sent his smoke up toward the mountain.

"Dave?"

Silence. And I was thinking, OK. Fine. Maybe next visit. Maybe next year, I'll get in.

The following morning we headed out: he in his truck, me in my rental car. I trailed him into town as far as the elementary school, where he was due for his morning class. He parked his truck. I stepped out of my car. We were five, maybe seven feet apart, standing in the muddy parking lot. May as well have been a million miles.

"See ya, Mart," he said.

"See ya."

After a few moments, we moved in for the habit of a hug. Brief. He turned and I gave a feeble wave as I watched him walk into Fraser Elementary School.

Five weeks later, I was back in Colorado staring at David's backpack. It was propped behind the Grand County coroner's desk. It was bright red, a Patagonia label stitched to the flap. My mother was next to me, Kleenex clutched in her hand. It was very early in the morning. We had arrived from New York the night before and now we were sitting in folding chairs facing the coroner. Her four kids were smartly framed, neatly coiffed, in photos lined up along the edge of her desk.

"I need to go to my brother," I told her.

"I'm sorry," she said. "You're only allowed to view the body through a window. We are fairly certain it was a heart attack, snowshoeing at that altitude, but the medical examiner first has to sign—"

"Please," I said. "Just to take his hand. For a moment."

It felt utterly sensible and irrational at once—this sharp need to get to him as quickly as possible and see that he was all right. As if he were expecting me, as if I could actually help him in some way. And I realized I was desperate to reach him before he'd been fussed with. Before someone arrived and closed his mouth and smeared rouge on his cheeks. I wanted to touch him first, hold him as he was.

I knew that someone from the Denver mortuary was already on the way up to fetch Dave. It had all, to our very great surprise, been prearranged. My younger sister had told me to look in Dave's desk for papers, a will. That morning, inside his top drawer, I found a folder. On the first page was a letter with a beautifully designed heading printed in shades of blue and gray, a little bird flying upward—

Horan & McConaty.

Funerals—Cremation—Pre-Planning.

Dear Mr. Moran,

Thank you for your decision to prearrange with us, an important step in assisting your family at a time of need . . .

I studied the documents. Dave, it turned out, had signed up for a funeral plan more than two years prior to this death. He was not yet forty-one years old when he started making payments. There it was, all spelled out in triplicate, his authorization to withdraw $53.95 monthly from his bank account. He had ordered an urn. The type he'd chosen was scribbled there on the appropriate line: "Scattering Model. Slate Grey."

We appreciate the confidence you have shown by your decision to prearrange with Horan & McConaty . . .

. . . keep these papers in a place that would not be difficult for your survivors to locate.

One of the forms asked in bold:

Religion?

Dave had scribbled *catholic*, with a small *c*, followed by a large question mark.

There was also a life insurance policy naming my younger sister, Carolyn, and her two children as beneficiaries.

I stared at the file of papers, the signatures and figures, stunned. I was well past fifty and it had never once occurred to me to make any such preparations. I held it all in my hand—the forms, the folder—picturing Dave walking into Horan's (we had known this lovely family since our parochial school days) amazed at his . . . what? Prescience? Practicality. His thoughtfulness. His sense of fate?

I showed it to Mom. She read it and, shaking her head, said, "Our little David did that. Imagine."

The coroner is sliding papers now, one by one, across to Mom, who picks them up and studies them. I glance over at the blur of text: a list, "Personal Effects," and a report, "Rocky Mountain Search and Rescue."

Mom peers at the list and reads aloud:

"Pocketknife, Tic Tacs, lighter, crucifix, pipe . . ."

She pauses.

"I didn't know your brother smoked a pipe."

Between the coroner and me there's the flick of a grin, which Mother catches, and the coroner says, "Ma'am, not to worry. Marijuana is pretty standard around here. The cops just tossed it."

Mom nods.

I keep looking at Dave's pack and then at the coroner. What a job, I think. Facing people like us who've arrived at eight in the morning, jet-lagged and grief-stricken, come to her small town at nine thousand feet to claim the body of a loved one. She's talking quietly now, as I remain insistent about going to him. "Let me just say," she counsels, "that, you may not want to see him . . . this way. You may not want to overpower your memories."

Mother nods, dabs Kleenex to her eyes. I can see that she's frightened by what she might see. As am I, but I'm determined to hug his shoulders, to see that he's in one piece.

We are all quiet for a time. From beyond a small window comes the occasional whoosh of traffic. I glance out to see cars and trucks traveling the main street, US 40, headed east toward Denver or farther west up and over the Continental Divide. There's a statue of a moose across the highway, propped in front of the Moose Café, large and waxy looking. The snow-mantled peaks of Rocky Mountain National Park rise up beyond, surrounding the immense valley in which we sit.

. . . one big hug from God . . .

"I need to go to him," I say to her again. "Please."

She talks of legalities, the ruling out of "foul play," the policy regarding the death of a person within a national park. I stare at her. Our eyes meet over the rim of her glasses. Finally, she leans forward,

"OK, look, it's early. This is just between us. OK? I'll go arrange things."

She steps out and down a long hallway. I turn again to the window. A Union Pacific train is making its way east, the clatter of its cars audible, compartment after compartment filled with goods for the living. The words *Union* and *Pacific* repeat past the glass. Mom and I sit silent in the little room—just the desk, some filing cabinets, the coroner's kids smiling up at us from their school portraits.

Suddenly she's back. She gestures toward a hallway.

I stand and look to Mom, who shakes her head, presses Kleenex to her face.

The hall is built of yellow brick lit with fluorescents that gleam along the linoleum floor. I pass a door to a large garage. Through the small window I glimpse vehicles lined up: a snowplow, an ambulance, and other emergency equipment. I pass a restroom, a storage closet, a drinking fountain.

I round the corner and the first thing I see is his right arm. Then all of him, his body resting on a gurney beyond a glass window, propped in front of a beige curtain like some diorama: *Sleeping Hiker. 2009.*

His sleeves are rolled up to the bicep, his skin red-colored. Sun- or windburned? Or just cold from the morgue, from the mountain? There's a white tag around his wrist. He is clothed just as he was when he had fallen, it appears. Lying there in full gear as if ready to get up from a nap and continue hiking. A blue plastic sheet, a kind of tarp, is folded back across his torso toga style, or like the turning down of the bed for a hotel guest—from right shoulder to left hip, covering half of his Patagonia vest. It occurs to me how the coroner must have taken him out of the fridge, rolled him here, and readied him just so for my viewing. I can see a wall of large drawers in the space just beyond, like the autopsy room in a scene from *Law and Order*.

I step closer to the window. His Patagonia boots are sticking up, attached to Patagonia knickers. I can see now written neatly in blue ink on the white tag around his wrist:

8–27–65   4–27–09.

The first and last lines of a short story—the day he was born and the bright Monday afternoon (thirty-six or so hours ago, now?) when he was snowshoeing up Strawberry Trail heading for the High and Lonesome Hut. His pack stuffed with clothes, a boomerang, a kite, some weed. Pulling a sled, with Guinness and shish kebab for half a dozen pals. Co-workers from the restaurant where he worked.

"He was about a mile up the trail," his friend Matt had told me. "Me and my girlfriend had fallen behind and as we came up the slope we saw him lying in the snow. Facedown. At first we thought he was clowning around. We could see by his tracks that he had just pulled through a ravine and . . . he was just there. I did CPR as long as I could. We called the Forest Service right away. It took them a while to get there."

He didn't know what hit him, that's what everyone has said about his heart failure. Instantaneous. Painless? What, I wonder, in those final seconds, did he know?

Nothing?

Everything?

There is a door to the left of the window. The coroner has left it ajar. I step in and around to Dave's side. His mouth is open in the shape of an O, as if he's about to sing. There is one string of saliva, tiny bubbles attached, running from lip to lip. She'd warned me about the mouth, told me it was because of the tube the rescuers had used up on the mountain in an attempt to pull him back to life. She'd said it might be gruesome but standing next to him now, he's beautiful—his face all peace. His hair billowing every which way, as if the wind up there on the trail is still caressing his head. His vest, boots, knickers cling to his frame—the uniform of an alpine soldier, my Jeremiah Johnson brother. I take his broad shoulders; I run my hands along his sturdy frame, pressing, praying over every part of him. My bunkmate, my brother. I press my cheek to his.

"Thank you," I say. "Thank you for being my brother. Sorry for failing to be more. . . . Sorry. Dave, you look so peaceful. Is this what you wanted? Out of here so soon? What was it? Why were you so stuck? Why were you so angry? Why . . ."

Shut up, Marty.

His face, his freckles are speaking to me. His voice utterly present.

Sshhhh, Marty. Get a load of this. Gone. Gone from here. Get a load of this . . . shhhhh. Gone, Marty. Look. Do you see?

I stare down at him for a long time. I brush my hand through his hair and suddenly I know I have to get Mom. I want to tell her she can do this. We are given this.

She sits clutching her Kleenex and I walk right in and, I don't know why, but I bow to her like some Buddhist monk, my palms pressed in prayer. I bow and say,

"Mom. He is beautiful. It's OK. Come with me."

And she stands just like that, and I take her shoulder and we walk down the hall.

She is silent at first, stroking his head, and then she begins to moan.

"Oh, Oh, Oh." She keeps stroking his face and his hair, saying again and again, "I worried about you every single day. OK, I won't worry anymore. I'm sorry, so sorry."

And then she says,

"Oh my baby, my baby, my store-bought baby boy."

I am standing just behind, my hand on her shoulder. I have never heard these words and I ask,

"Mom, what is that?"

And she says through tears,

"When you were really little, I used to call you and Chris my homemade babies. I used to call your little sister Carolyn and David my store-bought babies."

It seems that Dave's eyes flutter, his lips. After a moment I ask,

"Hey, Ma, how much did he cost?"

And she wipes her eyes and says,

"One hundred and fifty dollars." And she bursts out laughing. A sweet, sad laugh, and adds, "From Catholic Charities."

And when we finish our laughing and crying, we each lean down and kiss his forehead.

We wait for the hearse to come, all paid for by Dave, of course.

I watch the man, gray-haired and dressed in a black suit (dead ringer for the grim reaper), take Dave and roll him down the hall. I follow and observe as he loads him into the back of the hearse. As if reading my thoughts (thoughts he's no doubt encountered before), the man says, "We will take good care of him." And he shuts the door and drives away.

It was that night that I found the first of several of his journals. It was on his bed, a green Mead notebook, buried amid a pile of half-opened books tangled in his blanket and bedsheets. Sheets still replete with the smell of him.

Frank McCourt's *Teacher Man. The Tibetan Book of Living and Dying. Keats: A Life.*

Huge novels on his nightstand, novels he often spoke of.

Infinite Jest. One Hundred Years of Solitude. There was an enormous Jasper Johns poster on the wall above his bed. The yellow orange blue explosion of an abstract map of the United States. I remembered then, when he bought the poster on a visit to Manhattan. On a day we went together to the Museum of Modern Art.

I opened the notebook. On the first page I turned to he'd written,

Words to look up.
Trochaic
Inamorata
Didactic
Saturnine
Linnets
Infelicitous
Succor
Rodomontade
Bowers
Maudlin
Perspicacity.

I kept leafing through. It was filled with lists and poems and diarylike entries, some neatly printed and other pages written in

furiously wild cursive, hard to read. I came upon a long section
where he'd been camping and had written,

> *To the angel and spirit guides, please come and share your words*
> *and thoughts with me!!*

What followed were pages and pages of questions written by
Dave with answers written by . . . Dave.

Q *Are my spirits and angels with me?*

A Yes, young one we are always with you.

Q *Do you energies (should I call you this?) do you have any*
connection with the spirit of flies and mosquitoes? If yes, can
you ask them to leave me alone for a while?

A Young one they are fragments of the One Spirit. We will
try to see if they will let you be.

Q *Is there a spiritual consciousness for the world's population?*

A Young one you are so inquisitive. This question has
many aspects but suffice to say yes there is a spiritual
consciousness. The power and brilliance is
staggering. . . .

Q *Is this consciousness on the side of greater good?*

A Oh young one you care so much about the balance of the
world as a whole and this is admirable but do not be
dismayed as pain is a fact of life and this unresolved pain
carries on into the spiritual world. . . .

Q *Are father's spirits about?*

A Yes Son! We are here and have been awaiting. Patience is the virtue of a writer and I have surpluses, there is so much to do in this extraordinary place that patience isn't required. When spiritual needs arise you just take care of them and there is no waiting and I still have not figured out how this works but it is beautiful . . .

Q *Dad, can you see me, where I am?*

A Your MOUNTAINS! . . . I like that you are camping out and working on issues of your life.

Q *Dad, do you feel at home there?*

A Yes, Son, I do.

Q *Hey Dad, is the term failure used where you are?*

I WAS WALKING ACROSS CENTRAL PARK, a cold afternoon in March of 2010. Winter hadn't released its grip: the sun bright above, the crunch of snow still underfoot.

My cellphone rang. I saw Siba's name and peeled off my gloves. "Hello?"

"*Monsieur Martin?*" His voice seven pitches higher. "Martin. Martin. I got asylum!"

He told me he cried like a kid, that his lawyer did, too, when the judge said the words: "Asylum granted."

"Siba, my God, that's the best news! We have to celebrate. What would you like to do? Maybe we could organize a dinner with some of your friends? Or go to hear some music?"

But there was one thing, he made clear, that he wished to do.

"Martin, I want to go to the Statue of Liberty and take a picture there."

I met him at noon on a sunny Saturday at the PATH station down near where he worked at the sandwich shop. Siba came with his housemate Abraham (who'd also recently been granted asylum), and the three of us hiked south to Battery Park, there to board the boat. There, among the huddled masses, yearning to get through security.

The engines fired up and you might have thought we were taking a trip to Tahiti or Thailand on that ten-minute ride across New York Harbor. Siba and Abe moved from railing to railing pointing at the shifting skyline, the wide water views of lower Manhattan and New Jersey.

When we landed, everyone swarmed swiftly off the boat and toward Lady Liberty. *La Liberté Éclairant Le Monde.* "Liberty Enlightening the World." That's her official title. The name bestowed by the French government when they offered her to us in honor of our independence. After many years in the making, in 1886 she was finally placed atop her pedestal upon the eleven-pointed wall of former Fort Wood.

Siba kept taking pictures with a camera he'd borrowed especially for this day. He asked me to take several photos as well from every possible angle—Siba and Abe standing under trees, sitting on benches, always overlooked by the Lady. I watched Siba's face as he posed for the camera. He had a way of fixing his features, opening his eyes wide, tilting his head just a little—a kind of self-conscious timidity mixed with excitement. It was like watching a kid's first visit to, I don't know, the Grand Canyon? Disney World, The Statue of Liberty! Theirs was an infectious exhilaration made all the more sweet by the weight of what they'd endured, by the reprieve they'd been given. They'd won a new home and their faces were beaming with it.

Siba kept stopping and pointing at various aspects of the statue. "What's that?" he asked, his focus toward Lady Liberty's feet. There, under her left foot, was something I had never known of or noticed: a broken shackle.

We turned to a ranger wearing the familiar hat and uniform, a dark-haired fireplug of a guy. His nametag said Brad.

"Sir . . . Brad, what does that stand for?" we asked.

He pointed and said,

"That represents the smashing of tyranny."

Siba and Abe were full of questions; I translated.

"What are the spikes on her head?"

"They represent the seven continents."

What's that crown?"

"It's called a diadem."

"How much does she weigh?"

"Oh, about seven tons, or thereabouts."

"What's the tablet?"

"Keystone with the date of the Declaration of Independence. See the Roman numerals?"

Ranger Brad proceeded to tell us how he'd been in love with the Lady ever since he first saw her image on TV when he was a kid in Cleveland and that he knew one day he'd work right here. He gazed up toward the torch and said,

"It takes courage to fight for liberty."

It seemed he was referring to getting out of Cleveland.

Abe said, "I saw her on TV, too, when I was a boy in Cameroon."

"What does liberty mean to you?" Brad asked.

We were silent.

"Seriously, guys."

Abe and Siba smiled and inquired if they could take a picture with him. I served as photographer. Abe asked if he could wear Brad's ranger hat. "Yes" was the answer and Siba said,

"Martin, this is the best day of my life. Besides the day my son was born and the day I got asylum." He grinned and opened his arms wide. "You see, Martin? You see? Paradise."

We headed back into the city and ate dinner at Elephant & Castle, a comfortable old joint in the Village. Over salmon and cokes we chatted.

"Martin, you wasted a whole day with us," they said at one point.

"Don't say that," I said. "You can't imagine what a good day."

They began to sing snatches of English songs they'd memorized. Quietly, at first, then a little louder, sad pop tunes that rendered them utterly delirious. A nearby family kept looking over and cross-table conversation began.

"Where are you gentlemen from? How long have you been here?"

There was a little girl and her father took out his iPhone and brought up a map of Africa. A geography lesson ensued: Cameroon, Sudan, Senegal. The girl said,

"My grandma's from Sicily."

Another table got involved and asked if Chad was near Togo. The dad made the shape of Chad bright red on his phone and held it up for everyone in the restaurant to see. Siba called out,

"That was my home."

The little girl pointed at the puzzle piece half a world away and went back to her spaghetti.

When we stepped outside, Abe dashed across the street to a video store in search of a John Wayne film. Siba and I sat on the corner of Greenwich and Seventh avenues near a tall chain-link fence that was covered with memorial tiles to the lost and fallen of 9/11. We watched traffic, sipping cranberry Vitamin Waters we'd grabbed earlier at a swanky deli. Siba asked me what was in the water.

"Oh, electrolytes, nutrients."

"But three dollars a bottle? Why would anyone buy it?"

He burst out with that laugh, that bright laugh of his.

And I had to ask. And I finally did.

"Siba? Aren't you angry?"

He looked at me.

"About what happened to you? Your whole life is changed. I mean: do you hate them for what they did? Are you angry?"

"No, I'm not."

"Really? I am."

"Martin, it's like it was an accident. That's how I think of it. I was there in that place and that time. It happened, and . . ."

"And what?"

"*Ils sont,*" they are, "*analphabète.*"

"*Analphabète?*" I asked. And he explained.

"It means no . . . no words. Illiterate. Ignorant. Those men, most of them, they grew up with nothing. The army recruits them. I got to go to the city, school. I'm angry sometimes, but they . . . they don't know what they are doing."

He took a sip of water.

"But you must think about your family all the time," I said.

"I carry them with me but I can't think about them all the time. I need to live. If I grieve all the time I will . . ."

"Go blind?"

I left Siba and Abe on the corner of Christopher Street to walk to the PATH station and watched them, taller than most, as they melted into the Saturday evening throng.

HE WILL SLIP FROM MY LIFE OR, more accurately, move further into his. It happens slowly, in stages. Talking on the phone becomes rare. His days are full and so are mine and when I think of calling, sometimes I find his phone's been disconnected. I'm unable to reach him until he calls letting me know he ran out of minutes or has a new number or switched phone companies.

"Best to call Sundays, the day off," he tells me.

Weeks and even months go by. Sara tells me not to worry, that this is the way of it, Siba is finding his American path, speaking the language, discovering new work, new friends. "It's the natural course of things; there's a network of fellow immigrants out there who know the ropes. He's connecting with them, finding his feet, creating a life. He's putting what happened behind him."

"I guess that means me, too?"

"This isn't about you, Marty."

"Really? *It's not?*"

My phone rang one day. It'd been I don't know how long and there it was, his bright familiar singsong.

"Monsieur Martin?"

"Siba? How are you?"

"Good, good."

He asked about my mom and sisters. To my delight he asked it all in a very sure English.

"They're fine," I told him.

"Oh that's good. And how is your friend?"

"Henry?"

"Yes."

I'd always been rather discreet with Siba regarding my personal life. I can't name *exactly* all the reasons for this. A real and imagined cultural divide? My sense of maintaining a certain formality? Or, perhaps, it simply comes down to my own ancient and stubborn homophobia. I recall a Thursday evening at the International Institute; Game Night, they called it. I was playing Scrabble (in English) with Siba and a group of other African refugees. One of the guys set down the word "queer" on the board. Good for a whole lot of points. I was suddenly nervous but no one, it seemed, thought much of it except for one young man who asked, "What does that mean?" "Different or weird, right?" one girl said. And I thought to myself, well, here's the perfect opportunity to share a wider definition of *queer*—Exhibit A, standing right here, the white guy who sucks at Scrabble. Hello. But I was uneasy and let it pass. In any case, often enough through the months of our friendship, I had spoken to Siba about my friend Henry—"the man that I live with"—and at some point I noticed Siba added Henry to his list of my people to inquire about.

"He's doing well," I answered. "Thankfully he has work these days. And you, Siba? How is work? Are you still in school?"

"No school right now. I am working at a gas station. It's a good job."

"That's great."

"Martin, I am in Ohio. Cleveland, Ohio."

"Oh my gosh, no kidding?"

"Kidding?"

"Joking."

"No, no Martin. No *kidding*. I moved. I am living in Ohio. I have a friend who came to the US a few years ago. He is from

Cameroon. He's been living out here for some time. He has a house and a car. One day I will get a car. You *need* a car in America. My job is far. I take two different buses to work. I get up so early, Martin. But it is a good job. The people are good."

Weeks went by. We spoke again and he told me that he got his driver's license and he was saving for a car, that he had a second job valet-parking for a big restaurant. "It's easier to save money here in Ohio. Things are not so expensive as in New Jersey. I want to send money back home if I can."

I asked then about his family and he told me that he had finally had contact and knew that they were OK, though his mother had been ill and he was worried about her. He will have to move through many more legal steps before he can even visit Africa, let alone bring his wife and child here. "My wife wants it to be happening faster. I tell her to be patient. I am not sure she understands."

"Must be difficult."

"It is. I try to explain to her but . . ."

He trailed off.

"Do you like Cleveland?" I asked.

"Yes. But it is so cold. Cold like New York and . . . more snow! You know, Martin. I do not like the cold," he said, chuckling. "One day I will find someplace warm. I do miss New York. I miss my friends at the institute. I miss you, Martin. And Sara. I will visit. I will see you again one day."

"I hope so. I think of you a lot. I . . . I've started writing a new play and maybe a book, and part of what I'm thinking and writing about is you. About how much I've learned from meeting you, how grateful I am."

"Really? What is the book about?" he asked.

"I'm not sure. At first, I thought it was mainly about anger. Maybe? How anger is important and yet how some people are stuck on what has happened in their life and others not so much and . . . and . . ."

I stopped talking. Didn't have the words in English, let alone French. I never seem to know where it is I am headed in my work, much less how to describe it.

"Siba, it has something to do, I think, with understanding rage and compassion, about how they coexist. Or maybe a larger question really about . . . forgiveness? About realizing that I is . . . we."

I stuttered to a stop again. He was quiet.

I continued. "Our time together has made me think a lot about . . . loss and change. In writing about you I suppose I'm writing about myself."

More silence. I was worried, I realized, that he may be uncomfortable about all this.

"You there, Siba?"

"Yes. Maybe my English will be good enough one day that I can read what you have written."

"I hope so. Or I can read it to you."

Silence again. I found myself wondering if he recalled the day when he taught me the word *analphabet*. When he'd described his torturers as uneducated, unaware. His clear expression of compassion, "they don't know what they are doing," had struck and stayed with me.

Not long ago I was reading a passage from Thich Nhat Hanh, a Vietnamese Buddhist monk, when I tripped upon his definition for analphabet: "Hearts who cannot yet see." Immediately, I thought of Siba. His clarity of sight.

Across the wire came his voice asking,

"What kind of car should I get, do you think?"

"I have no idea. I've never had a car."

"No. No car?" He gasped. "Ever? Martin, you are not American!"

"I'm a New Yorker."

He laughed again and said, "I will get a used one. There are a lot of ads in the paper."

He began to speak of the large streets and houses and yards and all the cars and shopping malls. And snowdrifts. The nice Ohio people, and then,

"Good-bye, Martin. Talk soon. Tell your family hello from me."

TWO YEARS AFTER DAVID'S DEATH I found myself back in Fraser. It was summer's end. I'd forgotten how plentiful and miraculous the Rocky Mountain wildflowers can be this time of year. Everywhere the hills dappled with dazzling colors—fairyland.

I stayed with Ingrid. David had rented a room in her home for nearly five years. She's a generous and easygoing woman and they had become close. Helpmates. I was so glad that he'd had her near in what turned out to be the last years of his life.

I told her that I was going to hike Strawberry Trail up to where, once the snow had melted, we'd placed a bench in Dave's memory.

"Great," she said. "I have another suggestion, too."

"What's that?"

"Let me show you the spot where David camped just after your dad died, when he first got here and had no place to live. He showed it to me once. It's just a bit south of here, off Tipperary Creek, Tipperary Trail."

I loved the sound of that—Irish tripping off the tongue.

It wasn't a long hike: less than a mile up a narrow path winding through lush grass and a blanket of blooming flowers. Ingrid, an avid alpinist, had lived in Fraser for decades. As we climbed she kept nodding her head and pointing, identifying *every* living thing. Her knowledge was astonishing. It was like walking with Lady Audubon. She named things quietly at first, as if talking to herself, as if checking up on old neighbors.

"Ah, figwort. Skunk cabbage. Paintbrush."

I asked and pointed, embarrassed at all I'd forgotten since my Boy Scout days.

"And that?"

"Horsetail. And harebells. Oh, look, aster."

She seemed a goddess rechristening the world, reminding me to open my eyes and see it. Her long blond hair flecked with light, her voice calm as if in prayer—

"Columbine . . . daisies, your brother loved daisies, Queen Anne's lace . . ."

She stopped.

"See these?"

She knelt down and plucked six teeny tiny berries from amid a moist patch of green leaves.

"Here," she said.

She placed the little kernels into my palm.

"Pop these suckers right into your mouth. All at once."

It was an explosion of sweet and fresh on my tongue.

"Like jelly," I said.

"Wild strawberries. Jam straight from Mother Earth."

She ate a handful as we walked. Our fingers were stained red. We hiked on and up, winding through the aspen and birch and lodgepole pines.

"Here it is," she said.

It opened before us, a little Shangri-la. An emerald space perhaps forty yards long encircled by spruce and juniper and aspen, too. And speckled with flowers of purple and yellow hew. The creek wasn't visible but tucked just beneath a nearby ravine. The tune of it, the soft tippling of the water, played.

Ingrid pointed to a spot toward one end of the clearing, tucked forward near a tall patch of pines.

"He put his tent right here. He could walk over and get his water. See? And he parked his truck on the county road where we came in, not that far. He'd go into town and get groceries, use the Internet. That's when he found me. When he answered my ad for the room."

I walked over and down a small slope to the edge of the stream. The flow was narrow here, and swirled in small pools, tumbling over mica-flecked rocks. The water was perfectly clear. I scooped some and splashed my face. Took a drink. I walked back to the patch where Dave's tent had been pitched and lay down in the thicket of green. This is where his body slept. A home of his own, not a soul but Earth knowing where he was.

"How long did he live here?" I asked.

"About a month, I think."

We were silent. The creek talked. The wind answered. I lay there and listened.

There is a cure—listen, listen and allow nature to quiet the mind to hold you in her hand and cover your being with sights, sounds, smells, textures, and tastes. Breathe. This is where we belong.

Ingrid walked away and left me alone.

Dave was woven everywhere. Into earth, gone to sky, gone to seed. And I knew, absolutely knew, that he'd guided me, that he meant for me to see this exact place at this exact moment. He'd camped here in this very season, the height of summer, with the hope of having found his home. I remembered him telling me about this time. How dear it was to him to be alone in the woods. He'd not shown it to me while he was living. *Best you see it now,* his whisper was close and I whispered back,

Dave. Dear David. Thanks for leaving word . . .

Ingrid returned and stood near where I was stretched on the ground. We stayed silent for a long time. Then she said,

"See those?"

I sat up and turned to her.

"Which?"

"The taller blue flowers on either side of you, the ones peeking up past the thistles? There and there?"

"Oh, yeah?"

"You know what those are called?"

"Nope. Pretty ignorant. So much I don't know."

"Wild forget-me-nots."

I SAW SIBA ONE LAST TIME. Our meeting was far from New York and came about, as things often do, by chance. It was Christmastime and we finally, after leaving holiday messages, connected by phone. I told him that I would be leaving town for most of 2011 for a touring job and was glad to reach him before I took off.

"A goat?" he asked. "You're playing a goat?"

"Yes." I replied. "It's true. Can you believe it?"

I explained that I would be traveling to eleven cities across the Northwest, Southwest, and Canada. That I'd be playing the role of a teacher in a national tour of a Broadway musical called *Wicked*. A friendly goat who talks and, as it happens, can carry a tune.

"But, sadly," I said, "I won't be going anywhere near Ohio."

And he said,

"Martin, I am living in Houston now!"

"Texas?"

"Yes, Texas."

"My God, Siba, you get around!"

His life was changing fast in the months between our conversations. He explained that someone he knew had lived in Houston for a while and he was able to join his friend there. He had found a good job at a big hotel, valet-parking.

San Antonio was one of the cities on my tour. A morning's drive from Houston. Before Siba and I wound up our holiday wishes, we had devised a plan that several weeks hence, on a Monday off from the show, I'd rent a car and make a visit.

Before I knew it, I was punching Siba's Houston address into the GPS. The weather was fine and the drive was simple—one direct road. When I pulled into the driveway of the sparkling hotel, he was out front in a snappy maroon uniform, standing among three or four other guys. I waved. There was his bright grin and,

"Martin! Monsieur Martin!"

He gestured like a flagman on the tarmac of an airport, showing me where to park. When I got out, he gave me a hug and, with great excitement, turned to introduce me to his co-workers.

"These are great guys, Martin. Great guys!"

Most of them were local, tall white guys with short hair, shiny teeth, and Texas accents. They all shook my hand warmly, a small and hospitable army in their maroon jackets and khakis. Clearly they were fond of their African co-worker. Siba shed his jacket and we took off in my car.

"Let's go to the mall," he said. "Why are you laughing?" he asked.

"It just sounds funny to hear you say, 'Let's go to the mall!'"

"I love the mall," he said.

We decided to eat outside. There were a lot of men in suits who appeared to be conducting midday lunch meetings. Siba pointed to a table in the sun and put on some cool, dark shades. "Got these on sale," he said. He wore a bright plaid shirt, some shiny sneakers. An American guy.

We caught up on news. He told me that his son had been sick but was doing better. He'd lost his mother a few months before. He spoke of it only briefly, tears springing to his eyes, and added that life for his family seemed to have calmed down. He said he was saving, trying to send money to them but it was all so slow and his wife was growing frustrated. He worried about this. The time and distance was a growing source of tension. But the process, all of it, citizenship and papers and all the legal tangles, take a very long time. He just had to keep working hard, he said, and make more money to send home.

I asked about his health, if he had any insurance, if his head-aches were any better. They were and he'd been able to visit a doctor, but only one time. There were so many hurdles just to live, let alone find health care or insurance with his immigrant status. "But," he told me, "I got a car!"

After lunch we walked around the mall. Siba (who, even on a Subway-sandwich-shop budget always had a keen sense of style) kept eyeing the shops. We stepped into a clothing store. I happened to take an interest in a collection of white button-down shirts; I'd been meaning to grab one. Siba asked me if I liked them. Yes, they're nice, I said, and before I knew it, he snatched one up.

"Is this your size?"

"No, no, no need, Siba!"

He insisted.

I refused. "You are saving, for your family."

"I am with my friend," he said. "Please allow me to do this." He looked at me steadily. "My turn. OK, Martin."

He smiled the entire time we were at the checkout and handed me the package as we walked out of the store and past the sunlit sidewalks, past the many stores and cafés, and back to the car. He seemed so at home, so comfortable with it all.

Back at the hotel he proudly pointed out his car to me, a small Chevy. We said our good-byes. Over the next two years, after a handful of phone calls, I lost track of him. Those last con-versations were usually brief; he had a new job driving a truck out west, and time was money. He mentioned Utah and Washington

State and great snowstorms and mountain passes. He told me, "This pays the best yet. I am sending more money home."

When I walked away that day after we hugged good-bye and was about to get into my car, he called out,

"Martin!"

I turned to see his wide grin and, taking off his sunglasses, he said,

"Houston is the best."

And then he gestured upward.

"Look. I've found the sun."

AND SO, THE DREAM. . . .

The one I have been longing to tell you about.

It came to me not long after I'd taken Siba and Abe to Liberty Island. Not long after David left this world. It unspooled in the dark one night as Henry slept by my side.

It went
It goes
Like this:

I'm sitting at a table in a dimly lit restaurant. There's an older woman, two tables away, smoking a cigarette—thick sweater, red hair, lots of makeup. There's snow out the window and big-game animals on the walls: an elk with antlers, a cheetah, a bobcat baring its teeth. Is this a hunting lodge? I wonder. A stage set?

I notice then that sitting across from me is an old, pale man. Seems he has been there all along but I notice him suddenly now—in the unknowable logic that is dreamtime. I look closely at the man and it hits me. Oh Christ . . . it's *him*. Bob. The pale cheeks, the glasses, and a kink clutches at my stomach as somewhere from within comes a scream. Oh damn! *Not him again!* I've spilled enough ink on this guy to drown him, yet here he is, pasty as ever. And, well, dignified somehow as we sit together unpacking equipment from a red backpack: matches, a flashlight, a notebook, and then the small, framed photo of a child. I point to the picture.

"Is that you?"

Bob's quiet.

"Is it me?" I ask.

216

He shrugs.

Then suddenly the old lady yells out. She yells to Bob,
"Hey."

She's exhaling a lungful; the place is thick with it, like a scene out of *Gunsmoke*.

"Hey?" she yells again.

"Yeah?" Bob responds.

She stamps out her cigarette,

"So, tell me. What's the diagnosis after all?"

I feel a clench in my chest, the sense that the moment has arrived: *The answer* is coming!

Bob pauses and with great calm he states a series of four letters. Like Roman numerals on a keystone: "*CDLL.*"

My breath quickens. Oh my God, is this it? The cosmic key to crack the riddle? And the lady says,

"Oh, yeah? So what's that? Pedophilia?"

And Bob says, very calmly, in a sure and resonant voice,

"*No. Rehearsing Consciousness.*"

And my eyes snapped open—in real life.

Rehearsing Consciousness?

I sat up and flipped on the lamp next to the bed, the little one, not wanting to wake Henry, and ecstatic, I scribbled it all down. The scene, the weird, unknowable code and—I don't know why—*Rehearsing Consciousness*, the idea of it, *lifted*, released everything. The bed stand, Henry's Buster Keaton poster, my body, the whole place was *vibrating*. As if a door had swung open into this infinite electrified world where everything is *one*. This sense of rest. Like a Timothy Leary or Jack Daniel's moment but perfectly sober.

Exactly the same sensation I'd had that day in Africa at *The Cradle of Humankind*, when Tommy and I and all the others were staring at the map of Pangaea and Ruben said,

Welcome home.

And he'd described how bodies of land, our continents, fractured and drift back together.

When he said "*Welcome home,*" we'd all laughed—our little multicultural group, Swiss, African, Australian. We'd grinned at Ruben, at one another, suddenly sharing the air. I remember the Japanese couple bowed in my direction; I bowed back and we all walked toward the cave. Tommy was next to me. He'd insisted at first upon staying in the car. That's the way it's always done. But it was our last day together and I'd cajoled him to join the tour. He was next to me with his cellphone in the air, snapping photos.

"I didn't even know this was here!" he kept saying. "My wives will never believe this."

We started toward the cavern, out there in the blue middle, the wild terrain where human begetting began. I half expected to see ancestors of ours crouched at a fire grunting about the hunt. I stepped down into the earth and everything was humming, *joined.*

Maybe certain moments it just rises up like this, a little reminder amidst all the rage. "Hey look, we're of a kind; we share a cradle. The current of it running through every hour, the science of it ringing in our bodies."

Maybe that's what happened when I found Bob at the hospital and my hand reached across to squeeze his slumped shoulder. Maybe that's what happened on the morning of Dad's funeral.

When a murderous arm moved toward Barbara. There was the sun across her cheek and my hand, the *bones*, reaching over to touch as if rehearsing a memory, a sixth sense, conscious for an instant: wow, here is flesh of my flesh.

Lo and behold.

ACKNOWLEDGMENTS

All the Rage first took shape as an eighty-minute solo piece for the theater. I am ever indebted to those who helped bring it to the stage, as well as to those colleagues who helped me wrangle it into fuller form onto the page. My thanks to editor Amy Caldwell, who conversed and crafted patiently with me over many a year. My thanks to Seth Barrish, a sublime director and ever-generous friend, and to my intrepid literary agent, Malaga Baldi. Great appreciation goes to Dr. Sara Kahn, who guided me to the International Institute of New Jersey. I will be ever grateful to the refugees and asylum seekers whom I met and worked with at the institute. To be in their presence was a privilege and an enduring blessing. For reading and commenting upon the earliest drafts, my undying thanks to Marie Howe, Kathryn Harrison, Genine Lentine, Catherine Chung, Jane Lincoln Taylor, and James Lecesne. For time to talk and space to write and love in spades, my gratitude eternal to Dr. Carolyn Tricomi, Cynthia Huntington, Chris Moran, Carolyn Moran, Nick Flynn, the Barrow Group, John Dias, Stephanie Coen and Two River Theater, Wendy vanden Heuvel and piece by piece productions, Rising Phoenix Repertory, Ellen McLaughlin, Martine Carroll, La Jolla Playhouse, New York Theater Workshop, Keith Reddin, Philip

Himberg and the Sundance Theater Lab, Patricia Sherman, Koshin and Chodo and the New York Zen Center for Contemplative Care, The MacDowell Colony, Randolyn Zinn, Ingrid Karlstrom, Marin Mazzie, Jason Danieley, Snug Harbor Productions, Eve Ensler, Joe Danisi and Naked Angels, Diane Wondisford and Music-Theatre Group, Dave Johnson, Steven J. Stone, Mark A. Schlegel, Dr. Paul Browde, Steve Schwartzberg, Jo and Steve St. Clair, Ken Russo, Michael McIntyre, Oliver Williams, Bruce Bouchard, Steve Lepore and 1in6.org, and Paul Mason Barnes. To John Moore, the passionate journalist, who did more than he could ever know to spark the continuing inquiry. And, finally, to my dearest life—my husband and beacon, the man who has been dreaming next to me for thirty years, Henry Stram.

A note: The International Institute of New Jersey sadly, after nearly one hundred years of service to immigrants, closed its doors in 2012. It has left a void, but there are other great organizations doing the important work of helping refugees. The International Rescue Committee is always in need of support (go to Rescue.org), and a group I've come to know and especially love is the Refugee & Immigrant Fund. They are doing vital work with asylum seekers in the New York metropolitan area. If you'd like to learn more or be of help, please go to RIFnyc.org.

Also, a vital resource for men, and those who love them, seeking help or guidance around issues relating to childhood sexual abuse can be found at 1in6.org.